LIFE STRATEGIES FOR TEENS

Jay McGraw

A Fireside Book
Published by Simon & Schuster
New York   London   Toronto   Sydney   Singapore

FIRESIDE

Rockefeller Center

1230 Avenue of the Americas

New York, NY 10020

Copyright © 2000 by Jay McGraw

All rights reserved,

including the right of reproduction

in whole or in part in any form.

FIRESIDE and colophon are registered trademarks

of Simon & Schuster, Inc.

Designed by Interrobang Design Studio

Art direction by David Singer

Interior illustrations by Benjamin Vincent

Manufactured in the United States of America

10 9 8 7 6 5 4 3 2 1

Library of Congress Cataloging-in-Publication Data is available.

ISBN 0-7432-3288-7

I DEDICATE THIS BOOK TO:

JENNIFER McGOUGH FOR THE UNENDING LOVE AND CARE THAT MAKE HER NOT ONLY THE BEST POSSIBLE GIRL-FRIEND BUT ALSO A WONDERFUL BEST FRIEND;

MY GRANDMA JERRY FOR ALWAYS MAKING ME FEEL SPECIAL;

MY PARENTS FOR RAISING ME WITH LOVE AND UNDER-STANDING;

MY BROTHER, JORDAN, FOR WHOM I HOPE THIS BOOK SAVES A LOT OF TROUBLE.

ACKNOWLEDGMENTS

I WOULD LIKE TO EXTEND SINCERE AND LOVING thanks to my girlfriend, Jennifer McGough, the rock on which I leaned throughout this adventure. Thank you for your daily support, both editorially and morally. You have contributed not only to the quality of the book but also to my experience writing it. Thanks, Niff. I love you.

I would also like to thank my parents. Thank you, Dad, for always helping, supporting, and believing in me. Thank you specifically for your support and your belief in me to accomplish this task. This support and belief, of course, came as no surprise, but they are always valued. I couldn't ask for more. Thanks, Dad.

Mom, although I talk primarily about Dad in this book, you have been an equally strong influence in my life. Thank you, Mom, for all that you do, and for your support of me in all that I do.

I extend a heartfelt thank-you to my agent, Jan Miller, and her staff. From day one Jan has continuously gone well beyond what was to be expected. Thanks, Jan, for your help and your friendship.

I am most grateful to my editor, Dominick Anfuso, for his sacrifice and dedication, which undoubtedly made this a better book. Dominick, your work ethic is unrivaled, and your friendship is valued. I very much enjoyed working with you.

I thank Skip Hollandsworth, a truly gifted man. Thank you, Skip, for the time, talent, and dedication you poured into this book. You have definitely improved it, while at the same time you have made me a better writer. Thank you.

I thank Melodi Gregg for her unflagging willingness to work late and on weekends transcribing the manuscript. Thank you also for your patience in deciphering my chicken scratch.

Thanks to David Singer, the book's art director, and Benjamin Vincent, the book's illustrator. Thank you for your patience while working with the most uncreative, yet picky people ever. You are both true professionals and have contributed not only to the entertainment value of this book but also to its message.

Thanks to Jonathan Leach for taking the time to teach me to write in the first place.

Thank you, Bill Dawson, for always treating me with respect and for looking out for me as if I were a son.

Thanks to Andy Lawrence and Mike Ginn for their reading of and feedback on the early draft of the manuscript. Thanks also to Andy for his support during any ongoing project.

I would like to thank Mr. and Mrs. McGough for supporting me and recharging me with the homemade dinners. Thanks also to David McGough, Jr., for reading the manuscript and making suggestions for improving it.

Thanks to my brother, Jordan, for his input on the manuscript. Thanks also for making me laugh. Jordan, you are a perfect brother.

Thanks to my Grandma Jerry for being the best possible grandma.

I would like to thank my godfather, Gary Dobbs, and my Uncle Scott Madsen for always looking out for my best interests and supporting me and encouraging me in everything I choose to do.

Thanks to Brent Dobbs and Scott Madsen, Jr., for their lifelong friendship and support.

Thanks to Cherlynne Li for her talent in designing the perfect cover for this book.

Thanks to all of the focus-group participants. Your input and discussions truly shaped the initial direction of the manuscript. Thank you for your time and participation.

I would also like to thank executives Carolyn Reidy and Mark Gompertz at Simon & Schuster for their interest in this project and the expertise and passion they have shared with me.

Finally, I would like to thank Jennifer Love, Kristen McGuiness, and Jonathon Brodman of Simon & Schuster's editorial staff for all their hard work.

CONTENTS

FOREWORD

by Dr. Phillip C. McGraw

*I*N THE ORIGINAL *LIFE STRATEGIES,* MY NUMBER-ONE Life Law was You Either Get It, or You Don't. It hardly seems fair for that law to come back and haunt the guy who wrote it, but come back it did. When the discussions for *Life Strategies for Teens* got under way, my son Jay said, "Dad, trust me, when it comes to teens, *you don't get it!*" He told me that he had, in fact, learned and applied a tremendous amount of my teachings in general, and the laws and messages in *Life Strategies* in particular. The problem was, according to Jay, that it took him most of the six years that he was a teenager to translate and plug those laws into his young life.

I can tell you that while it may have taken Jay six years, he did get it done! My challenge to him was clear: If I don't speak "teen" and you do, if you have figured out how to express the importance of the ten Life Laws in terms teens can understand, then do it! You hold in your hands Jay's response to that challenge. I could not be more proud, yet humbled. His interpretation is powerful and inspiring. It is a message of self-determination and the power for all young people to create change, even though many of these teens may feel anything but in control of their lives.

Now, I have to tell you, if anyone had come to me when Jay was a sophomore in high school and said that within a very few years he would write a book on creating results at a young age, I would have laughed out loud. I would have laughed if anyone had said he was going to read a book that wasn't assigned, with his progress being monitored every fifteen minutes. But write it he did. Between then and now, something remarkable happened in this young man's life, and that something is the story of this book.

You see, in those few years, Jay figured out how to take what I was teaching adults and translate and apply it to life at a much younger age. He began to realize that he had tremendous power to influence his life through the choices he made and the goals he pursued. He apparently learned that while as a teenager many things in life are structured and perhaps even set in stone, there are a lot of other aspects of living that can be greatly influenced.

I watched this evolution from a boy, who, at best, merely tolerated school and went with the flow of life, into a young man who decided to rewrite the script of his life and use his skills and abilities to create success in his own life not after he became an adult, but right now. And to do it all while he was still having fun! As I marveled at this evolution, I was constantly wondering what was going on in this boy's mind. I now have my answer in the current book, *Life Strategies for Teens*. Jay truly did figure out life from a teen's point of view, and young readers will be blessed by the fact that he chose to write it all down.

He has taken the original *Life Strategies* and translated it into teen-speak.

I cannot describe the pride with which I introduce and endorse my older son's first book, *Life Strategies for Teens*.

If you are a parent, I can tell you that if you can get your own teenager to incorporate the insights and lessons of this book into his or her own thinking, feeling, and behavior, you will see the evolution

I have seen. If you are a teen reading these words, I can tell you that you are about to unleash a power of choice and self-determination that you never thought imaginable. Whether your challenges are with parents, peer pressure, a struggle for independence, or a desire to make a plan for your life, hang on, because you will be amazed by what happens next.

PROLOGUE

Dear Diary,

When did it all change? Everything is so different now. Mom was so much fun. We used to do everything together. I used to like school, I liked my friends, and everything was just so easy.

When did it get so hard? Was it when recess turned into study hall? Was it in junior high when we all started dating? It is like one day I felt free and the next day I felt pressure. I get so tired of worrying about what everybody else thinks. All of a sudden I feel so self-conscious. Who will sit with me at lunch? Will somebody talk about me behind my back?

My dad makes me feel like I've done something wrong because I want to date or spend more time with my friends. I'm always so irritated but I don't know why. I'm bored. Some of my friends seem so together, but I am just going day to day. I wish I could talk to Mom but she doesn't listen anymore. All she does is criticize.

She and Dad would kill me if they knew about the beer, but everybody does it except for the losers and the geeks. I guess it is fun sometimes but I hate how everybody gets so mad when I don't want to drink.

I wish I was either 10 again or 25, but this sucks. I wish I could just stay here in my room. It's lonely, but at least I am not downstairs getting interrogated about my friends and my grades. I'm going to be grounded for life when my report card comes out. Oh well, at least it's a good excuse not to go out drinking next week . . .

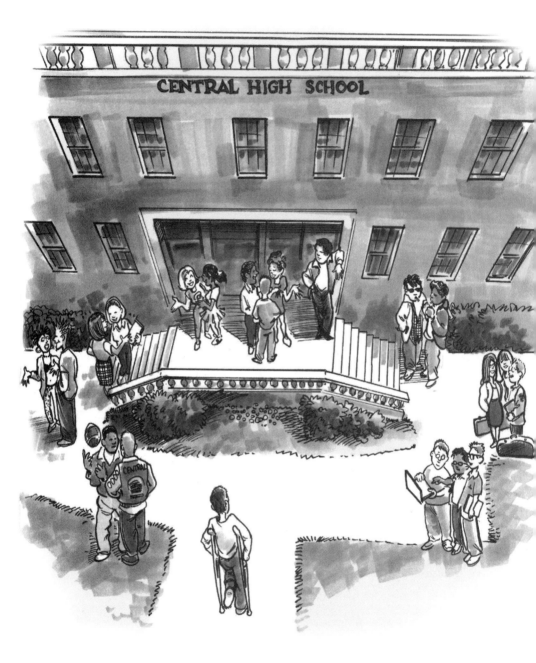

INTRODUCTION

To drift is to be in hell; to be in heaven is to steer.

—George Bernard Shaw

*I*JUST RECENTLY STOPPED BEING A TEENAGER, BUT just because I had a birthday that doesn't mean I don't still have to deal with many of the issues in the diary entry; and to be completely honest with you, if someone had handed me this book just a few years ago while I was in junior high or high school, I would have shaken my head in disgust and thought: "Yeah, right. Who are you kidding? You really expect me to read a book on being a better teenager? Come on, I don't even have time to read all the crap I'm already getting assigned to read in school! Read it yourself."

Are you thinking the same thing right now? Admit it. Your mom or dad or some well-meaning relative or friend has given you this book—or you bought it for yourself in a weak moment and you're already mumbling under your breath, "No thanks! This book is probably designed to help me be more of what parents and adults want me to be. It can't be designed to help me get more of what I want. No book writer could possibly know what I want. So nice try."

Are you as tired as I am of books constantly telling you the same old Brady Bunch, Beaver Cleaver, goody-two-shoes BS about doing your best to understand your parents, doing your homework, making curfew, getting a haircut, dropping that hemline, and blah blah blah? Books that have sentences that start with those five deadly words, "When I was your age . . ." Look, we don't live in Pleasantville and Opie would probably get the crap beat out of him daily in your zoo of

a lunchroom. So I have one word for a lot of the input both you and I get from school counselors, books, and articles: *borrring!*

So what's the deal with a book about Life Strategies? Strategies—smategies! If you are at all like me, you are just trying to get through the day without your parents snapping at you, or your geometry teacher flunking you, or some Neanderthal football player pushing you into the locker, or you're not getting anyone to pay attention to you because everyone is competing with or losing to Miss Popular. Why would you spend time jacking around with something called Life Strategies?

I'll tell you. The Life Strategies you're going to learn are all about getting you more of what you do want, and less of what you don't want in your life. This is a book for you—not for your parents, or teachers, or anyone else. I am not some know-it-all who's been everywhere and done everything—and neither are you. But between us, we are going to cover pretty much all of the possible problems. When I say Life Strategies, I simply mean coming up with plans for obtaining the things that matter to you, right now. Notice I said things that "matter to you." I'm betting you haven't had a better offer recently.

Now, because this is a book, I can't ask you specifically what it is that you want. But I have talked to a lot of kids from all over the place and I've asked them the "What do you want, what do you care about, what do you need?" questions. I am not sure what you would say, but here are some of their answers that might help you start thinking about what you really want:

Kim, age 16: "I want my parents to listen to what I have to say instead of interrupting me and telling me 'the answer is no' and 'it's for your own good.' Just hear me out, I might be right once in a while."

JP, age 13: "I want my parents to stop giving me a history lesson about how things were when they were teenagers. This is a different world with different problems so they should stop living in the past."

Daphne, age 18: "I want to figure out what I want to do with my life. I am bored; I've got no plan and no plan to get a plan. I'll be on my own soon and I'm starting to freak out."

Billy, age 18: "I don't really care about anything. There's just nothing exciting in my life. I couldn't care less about school, and I don't even care if I date or not."

Kerri, age 17: "Every adult in my life treats me like a two-year-old. I've made some mistakes, but God, it doesn't have to be a life sentence."

Jimmy, age 16: "I see other kids in school doing so well and I think, "What's the use? I'm not going to catch up to them, so who cares?"

Sharon, age 14: "I want the freedom to date! I have a boyfriend but my mom doesn't trust men because my dad screwed her over."

JT, age 17: "I am a senior and I should be having fun, but I am so obsessed with grades that I know my last year is just passing me by. My parents even tell me to have fun, but I just worry too much."

Sound familiar? Hit home? Do you relate to all or some of these statements? A lot of the people I talked to had really big problems answering that question, and you may, too. They were able to tell me what they didn't want, and what they were sick of in their life, but they couldn't say exactly what they wanted. Knowing what you don't want is important, because then you can identify the things you want to eliminate from your life. In fact, there were so many common answers to the "What don't you want?" question in the focus groups I conducted that I just put them in a list for you ("focus group" being fancy words for sitting in a circle and talking to a bunch of kids with opinions):

THINGS I HATE AND WANT TO ELIMINATE:

* ★   Zero control over my life
* ★   Parents who don't understand my life
* ★   Two-faced friends
* ★   Cliques that don't include me
* ★   Peers trying to get me to try things that I don't want to do
* ★   Hypocritical adults
* ★   No money, and no way to get money
* ★   No transportation
* ★   Feeling confused about what I want to become
* ★   Worry and pressure over grades and friends
* ★   Lack of confidence
* ★   My lazy lifestyle

TO READ OR NOT TO READ

So is that what you want? To be less than satisfied with certain aspects of your life? What is it you want to do to make your life better? What is it you want to do to make you feel that you're living with some passion and some kick-ass excitement, instead of being just another nose picker? What do you want to add to your life, and what do you want to eliminate from it?

Let me ask an even more basic question: Do you even think you've got the power to make big changes in your life to get what you want? Or do you think that because you're not yet self-supporting and on your own that you're pretty much stuck with what life gives you?

I promise you, you've got a lot more personal power than you know. You just aren't yet aware of how to use it. While it is true that you cannot control every aspect of your life, you are not powerless, and you are not trapped. You can influence major parts of your life much more than you could ever imagine. You can get more freedom and more control over what happens to you. You can live with the kind of confidence and enthusiasm that will make you stand out compared to everyone else in your school. You can set up your life in such a way so that your parents will no longer treat you like a little kid. You can command the respect of others, instead of feeling like they are controlling your feelings and your moods. You can set up your life so you'll quit worrying about your future and start creating it.

If all you want to do is bitch and whine about how lousy your life can be, then there's no need to read this book. If you want to believe you already know everything you need to know, stop reading. If you want to continue ignoring what power and influence is at your fingertips, then give the book away. Or you can let me save you a lot of time and trouble. I want to show you how you can take responsibility and make your life what you want it to be.

You are probably sitting there thinking, "Sounds great, but who are you to be talking to me, and how are you going to show me how to take control of my life?"

Good question!

I am Jay McGraw, a twenty-year-old college
student at the University of Texas. But to
really answer your questions, I am also
the son of Dr. Phil, the guy known as
America's Life Strategist, the guy Oprah
has nicknamed "Dr. Tell It Like It Is
Phil." Your parents probably know my
dad well; in addition to appearing on the
Oprah show about once a week, he writes
books teaching them how to improve their
life. In fact, he wrote the original *Life Strategies*.

My dad is a psychologist who has spent his whole life studying
human behavior. He is fascinated at figuring out why people do what
they do and don't do. He really analyzes things, top, side, and bottom.
Think of having to grow up with a dad like that! (I'm hoping you'll
join in a chorus of sympathy moans for me and my little brother!) He
really knew how to chap my ass sometimes, but I have to admit, all in
all, it hasn't been that bad of a deal.

Anyway, back to the original *Life Strategies*. My dad came up with
these ten Life Laws based on his years of experience and study, and he
claims that these ten laws determine everything that happens in your
life. Here they are:

1. YOU EITHER GET IT, OR YOU DON'T.

2. YOU CREATE YOUR OWN EXPERIENCE.

3. PEOPLE DO WHAT WORKS.

4. YOU CANNOT CHANGE WHAT YOU DO NOT ACKNOWLEDGE.

5. LIFE REWARDS ACTION.

6. THERE IS NO REALITY, ONLY PERCEPTION.

7. LIFE IS MANAGED; IT IS NOT CURED.

8. WE TEACH PEOPLE HOW TO TREAT US.

9. THERE IS POWER IN FORGIVENESS.

10. YOU HAVE TO NAME IT BEFORE YOU CAN CLAIM IT.

Those are the laws of life, the rules of the game. Those ten laws are going to teach you how to take control and get the things that you want.

You're probably thinking, "Oh my God, it took him his whole life to come up with those ten laws? They don't sound very fancy to me." But they aren't supposed to be fancy. They are just supposed to work, and they do. Whether you want a good-looking date, more freedom and respect from your parents, better friends, or whether you want to just feel good about yourself, these ten Life Laws will get that for you. That is what this book is about, getting the things you want out of life.

And isn't that the point? To get what we want in life. Unless your zip code is 90210 (and even if it is), we aren't living in a "fantasy land" here. We're not driving a BMW, or walking around with a body that would make the cast of *Baywatch* jealous. You and I have to deal with problems every day. We get food in our teeth, fight complexion problems, wear braces, get embarrassed by our parents, wake up with hair so happy it stands up to cheer, and then eat cereal while reading the box.

We have lives that are in an in-between state. If you are like me and all of my friends, you want independence above all else, sort of. But we also like being dependent, sort of. You've heard that old saying, "Be careful what you ask for, you just might get it." See if you can find yourself in this example:

Saturday 1:05 P.M.

Denise: "Mother! I am not a child! I am 15 years old and I don't need you running my life. I don't need you hovering all over me. Give it a rest!"

Saturday 6:15 P.M.

Denise: "Mother! Oh my God, you have to take me to the mall right now, I need ten dollars. I am out of mascara. And will you fix me something to eat? I am starving. Hurry up! Jason will be here in an hour! Oh, and can I borrow your earrings?"

I'll bet similar conversations go on around your house more than you want to admit. They sure do around mine. We want what we want when we want it and that's okay, but we have to be realistic, too. We want freedom to go and do, and freedom to make decisions for ourselves. But whether we want to admit it or not, it is nice to have ol' Mom and Dad around when we need them. Like when we need money, transportation, a roof over our head, or food to eat. With every privilege comes a price. Looking back, I sure wanted freedom, but I'm glad I had my parents to look after me.

Let's just be real honest: We want to run things, be independent and all grown-up; but the real truth of the matter is it hasn't been more than two or three years since we were playing with toys in the same room we now want to make out in. Not too long ago we were fantasizing about the Power Rangers instead of Yasmine Bleeth or Leonardo DiCaprio. It wasn't that long ago that we went to McDonald's and ordered a Happy Meal so we could get the toy and put it in our drawer with all of our Beanie Babies.

Face it: You're in transition, and you feel more like a child on some days and more like an adult on other days. You're tired of feeling as if you're drifting. You're tired of feeling so unmotivated. You really do want to make better grades, you want to get along better with your parents and people like your teachers, you want to make a good impression, you want to get a head start on the very competitive job market that you know is waiting for you out there—but you just aren't sure where to start. Your life is getting ready to start changing so fast you are not going to believe it. I am not ashamed to admit that I want a good life in every sense of the word. I want more stuff. I want more freedom. But I also want to be at peace inside, feeling good about my life and everything in it. I want a good life now, and a good life when I am an adult as well. But here is the key lesson I've learned—one that I want you to get big-time: You cannot "cram" for life. You can cram for a biology test. You can get *Cliff's Notes* and cram for a lit final, but you can't cram for life. Everything you will ever be, you are now becoming. It's okay to live in the moment, but the choices you are making now are the building blocks for where you will be later.

So I want this book to be about both now and later. I want this book to be about getting you what you want now, and setting you up to have what you want later.

To do that, you have to take charge of the things that you can influence, and you have to stop whining about the things you cannot. Face it: You cannot instantly get older, you can't beam yourself into the middle of Beverly Hills and some exotic life, and you can't change your parents. You can, however, start making things happen right where you are in Your Town, U.S.A. My English teacher used to say, "You have to bloom where you are planted." I always thought, "Shut up! Nobody talks like that." But he was right. We can bloom where we are planted. We can make our lives work right where we are.

YOU CAN'T WASTE ANY MORE TIME

I didn't just stumble into writing this book; I am on a mission. My dad was originally going to write *Life Strategies for Teens*. In fact, I was there when he was talking to his publisher about it. But living by Life Law Five, Life rewards action, I said, "Wait a minute. Hey, he's my dad and I love him. And I'm no moron but it took me years to unravel his version of the Life Laws; and when you are a teenager, you don't have years to burn. If somebody is going to write this for teenagers it needs to be me, not him. I've figured out what my dad is saying and can translate it so that people younger than thirty can understand it. I don't care how smart he is, he's forgotten a lot about what it means to be a teenager. He may have more graduate degrees behind his name than I've got letters in my name but my dad saw the first New Year's countdown that Dick Clark hosted. That's old!"

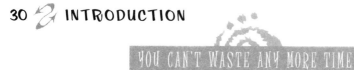

"Let me do the book," I said, "so it won't go over every teenager's head. Let me give them a chance to get what I wish I had gotten. Let me tell them in a way that they'll understand that there are answers to their predicaments, whatever those predicaments may be. Let me tell them that being a success and being a winner don't just happen. Let me tell them they can make it happen, and that it's easy to do if they just know the rules. Most important, let me make it clear that it is not too late. They can improve their lives, and they can redefine themselves."

That is what I hope I've done. When you get finished with this book, you'll know that even with all the restrictions put on you, you are not a passenger in your life. You are not a victim or a prisoner just because your parents currently control where you live, what you eat, what you drive, and how much money or freedom you enjoy. You have an incredible amount of power to choose so many things in your life that will dictate the outcome of your life. I know that when you get finished reading this book, you'll be astonished at all of the freedom you didn't know you had.

Bottom line: You are in control of your life in many ways that you do not know. You will be able to receive the level of trust and independence that you think you are capable and deserving of. You will reach that point of self-confidence where you will no longer be nervous around anyone in your life. You'll know that you'll have the inner strength to handle any predicament. You'll know that you have the tools to make the right choices to get the results you want.

If that's what you want, then great, because that's where we're going.

Now let's go. You're about to leave everyone around you standing in place.

LIFE STRATEGIES FOR TEENS

POWERING UP

The secret to success is to know something
nobody else knows.

—Aristotle Onassis

I MADE YOU A LOT OF PROMISES IN THE INTRODUCTION
and here's the catch: You have to make them come true. Let me
warn you right now, reading this book is not going to be a pas-
sive experience. This is not going to be like an English class lecture,
where you can doze off and not miss anything. It's not going to be good
enough to tell people at the end of this experience, "Hey, I read a book!"
The true test of the value of this book, or any other book, should be
whether or not it changes your life. Hold yourself to that standard.
Don't just mindlessly turn these pages and let things fly out of your
brain just as quickly as they flow in.

Remember, I was like that for a long time. I considered my dad's Life Laws sort of interesting. But I didn't consider them "real laws," the kind of things that I needed to deal with every single day.

To me, real laws were, "When you see a Stop sign, you'd better stop—or you get a ticket." Real laws were things like the law of gravity. If you step off the top of a building, you fall straight down and die. Hey, those were laws I understood. But I figured that when my dad went on and on and on (and on) about these Life Laws, he was just trying to discipline me. You know the way parents are.

Big, big mistake.

What I know now is that these Life Laws are in force all the time. Furthermore, when you violate these laws, there is a high price to pay just as if you break a criminal law and get caught by the police. When you violate the Life Laws, you very simply get what you don't want, and you don't get what you do want.

TAKING CONTROL: THE TEN LAWS OF LIFE

There is nothing more frustrating than trying to play a game when you don't know the rules, you don't know the objective, and you don't have the skills that you need to be good at the game. But everything is

easy when you know how. What I have figured out that I want to pass on to you is that life, in many ways, is a series of games that have rules and skill requirements just like any other game. I'm going to help show you how to play that game. I'm going to show you the rules.

This book, as I said earlier, is based on my dad's book *Life Strategies*. Even though my boring old dad wrote it—and I may not be totally objective—I've got to tell you, it is a great book. It is a particularly great book if you are about forty years old, married with 2.2 kids, have a career and a barking dog. If you're mainstream America, it's dead-on and ready to go. It is not a great book, however, if you are a teenager trying to get a foothold in your life. It is simply not written in a way that is relevant to us. But I will tell you something that I discovered: His ten Life Laws are relevant to us in a major, major way. If you are going to win this game, the game of life, you have to understand the rules of the game. You also have to know the penalties and rewards associated with breaking those rules. What the adult *Life Strategies* did was identify the rules. What this book does is translate them for you and me.

I've translated those Life Laws in such a way that it doesn't take you years to understand them. Let me again tell you what the ten laws are, but this time I will give you an idea what they mean to you and me:

THE TEN LAWS OF LIFE

1. YOU EITHER GET IT, OR YOU DON'T.

How to get the <u>L</u> for Loser off your forehead.

2. YOU CREATE YOUR OWN EXPERIENCE.

Become the star of your own life.

3. PEOPLE DO WHAT WORKS.

The truth about why you can act so weird.

4. YOU CANNOT CHANGE WHAT YOU DO NOT ACKNOWLEDGE.

Get big-time real about your shortcomings

and make a "to do" list.

5. LIFE REWARDS ACTION.

What are you waiting for? Get it in gear!

6. THERE IS NO REALITY, ONLY PERCEPTION.

Open your eyes and get into focus.

7. LIFE IS MANAGED; IT IS NOT CURED.

Keep it in gear, no coasting.

8. WE TEACH PEOPLE HOW TO TREAT US.

Don't be a doormat.

9. THERE IS POWER IN FORGIVENESS.

Your "get out of jail free" card.

10. YOU HAVE TO NAME IT BEFORE YOU CAN CLAIM IT.

I know what I want, and I want it now!

Even if you're thinking that all you want is a decent car, an incredibly cool date, and your parents off your butt, this is still the right book for you. Here's the deal: You are not going to get those things or anything else you think you want if you don't learn how this world works. Those ten Life Laws, which right now might seem to be about as pointless as the soil content in China, are in fact controlling the outcome of every single aspect in life.

If you know the Life Laws, then you'll know why your parents say no when they say no, and yes when they say yes. You'll know why certain teachers get under your skin, why some students treat you like dirt, and why on some days you feel so bad about yourself. You'll also know what to do about it. You'll be in control.

If you're not in control, then you're probably following the Ten Loser Laws of Life. These are the laws that keep you a passenger in life instead of being the driver. If you follow these laws, you're just another cow in the middle of the herd, getting pushed from side to side.

THE TEN LOSER LAWS OF LIFE

1. YOU JUST MAKE IT UP AS YOU GO ALONG.

There are no rules you can live by.

2. IT'S WRITTEN IN THE STARS.

For $4.95 per minute you can hear about your future.

3. THE DEVIL MADE YOU DO IT.

How to ignore the things that really make you tick.

4. DENIAL REALLY IS A RIVER IN EGYPT.

How to avoid change by avoiding your problems.

5. BE PATIENT; LIFE WILL EVENTUALLY DELIVER.

How to look out the window and hope it comes your way.

6. LIFE IS WHAT IT IS.

How to accept what you don't want.

7. GET IT RIGHT ONCE AND YOU ARE HOME FREE.

How to coast from the top of the hill.

8. PEOPLE ARE WHAT THEY ARE.

How to accept crummy relationships.

9. GET EVEN THROUGH GRUDGES.

You are just mad and there is nothing anybody can do about it.

10. LIVE LUCKY.

How to sit on the shore and hope your ship comes in.

I want you to stop living that list and start living the real laws of life.

These Life Laws will teach you how to be successful in the world. If you ignore them and stumble along, wondering why you never seem to succeed, you will cheat yourself out of everything you deserve. Successful life is nearly impossible if you have no knowledge of these Life Laws. So take the time to learn them, adapt to them, mold your choices and behavior to them, and you will consistently become more and more successful.

With these laws, you will also find that you have the tools to reach for something better for yourself. They will get you to a place where you can find out that real pleasure doesn't mean dabbling in drugs. They will teach you that real power doesn't mean occasionally popping somebody in the mouth with your fist. They will help you recognize that true affection is not having your girlfriend or boyfriend sneak over after your parents have gone to bed. Just like learning how to read, write, add, and subtract, you are now going to learn how to play the game of life—a game you very much want to win.

PLUGGING INTO THE SYSTEM

So if you're a typical skeptic—and I hope you are—then this should be your first question: "If these laws are so darn important, then why haven't I heard of them before?"

Well, you probably have heard some of the principles within these laws at one point or another. But I can almost guarantee that you have never heard the bulk of this information. Let me ask you this: Has anyone ever sat down with you to devise a complete "strategy" for your life? Of course not.

But don't blame yourself. It isn't your fault you don't have a life strategy. The truth is that you're probably like everyone else in this country. You haven't been taught anything about the way people work. You haven't been told about why we behave the way we do—and what we can do to alter that behavior. You have never been taught how to manage the emotions that can sometimes engulf you as quickly as a wave out of a typhoon.

Let's face it. Your teachers and parents weren't taught these Life Laws either. Those you entrust to prepare you for life aren't that prepared. (Of course, that doesn't keep them from jumping your ass when your life doesn't go well.) Oh, sure, in school you are taught when the War of 1812 was and you're taught who's buried in Grant's Tomb. But are you ever taught something important like what to do when your parents yell at you? You are taught how to do algebra, but are you taught what to say to yourself when you hear kids laughing behind your back? You are taught the scientific names of ten different plants in biology, but are you given a similar list of ten different ways to build your confidence? Did anyone ever teach you how to be heard by your parents, how to manage your anger, or how to create independence in your life?

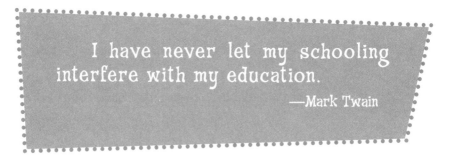

I have never let my schooling interfere with my education.
—Mark Twain

It's possible to learn what to do. You no longer have to think, as I once did, that you are being totally controlled by adult authorities and that you can't do a thing about it until you get out of school, or get out of your parents' house, or get your own place, and start a new life.

This is the best time possible to develop a life strategy. This is the time of life when you can build the foundation upon which you will launch the rest of your life. This is the time when you can learn the right way to stand up for yourself and learn to stand up *to* yourself. I know that statement must sound a little weird—and we're going to talk a lot more about this when we get to our first Life Law—but the biggest battles you must deal with right now are not battles with your parents, teachers, or any of your peers. They are battles within you.

START THINKING ABOUT WHAT YOU WANT IN LIFE

I'm not saying that your goal with this book is to have some career plan in place. But many of us have just stopped dreaming and we now simply react to whatever life deals us on any given day. The problem is, if you have no idea what you want, if you have no idea what your life would include and not include, it is almost impossible to make any kind of plan or live with any kind of purpose. Here is a promise you must make to yourself: You have to be willing to start wanting again, and that means identifying what it is that will make you happy.

Are you out of touch with your deepest dreams? In later chapters, you're going to be pushed to create a vision of who you want to be and how you want to get there. But the time to start thinking about it is now. This is the first of several exercises that can help you learn more about yourself. Have some fun with the answers.

MY POSSIBILITIES

1. WHO IN THE WORLD WOULD YOU LIKE TO SPEND A DAY WITH? WHY?

....

....

....

2. WHAT ARE THE QUALITIES THAT YOU ADMIRE MOST IN THAT PERSON?

....

....

....

3. HOW CAN YOU ACQUIRE THOSE QUALITIES FOR YOURSELF?

....

....

....

For a few moments, imagine yourself satisfying all of your possibilities with all of those qualities. How do you feel? Take a breath, clear your mind, and try to imagine that feeling. What would it feel like to embrace all your dreams and to actively work at living them out instead of daydreaming about them? What would it feel like to know you are fully tapping into your potential?

BE WILLING TO TAKE POSITIVE RISKS

Finally, here's the last promise you must make to yourself. You must be willing to change. Sound simple?

I didn't think so!

Isn't it ironic how adults like to say that teenage life is a period of experimentation? We know that's not exactly true, don't we? In reality, there are two types of experimentation. The first type we are all familiar with. We all have  experimented, or at least know someone who has experimented, with drugs, alcohol, and sex. Maybe you or your friends have dyed your hair pink, gotten a tongue piercing or a tattoo, and maybe you've even sneaked out of the house and so on and so forth. That's one kind of experimentation.

But when it comes to the second kind of experimentation, taking a real chance that can actually create significant change in your life, isn't it true that you are resistant to risk and change because it either seems too hard or you have a fear of the unknown? Instead of taking a risk to improve the quality of your life, you're satisfied with being an under-achiever, like Bart Simpson. You sit on your hands. You seem afraid—afraid of maybe not being immediately successful. Or you're worried that other people will judge you.

Think of the excuses you have used when you've debated with your-self about making a change:

★   "I'm not doing that bad."

★   "I am not old enough to worry about that yet."

★   "Hey, I see just as many problems with my classmates."

★   "I'm too busy with sports, school, or my hobby."

★   "If I change, the friends I have won't like me."

★   "I'm doing as well as half the class."

★   "Everybody who has pressured me to be different will think they have won."

★   "I'm trying, but it's so hard."

★   "Well, this is just how I am."

How pathetic are those excuses? All they do is keep you from being your best. I want you to remember the words of hockey legend Wayne Gretzky. "You miss 100 percent of the shots you never take." It's the same way with life. You've got to have the attitude right from the beginning that you are not going to stay in the place where you are now. You can't read this book and go, "Hmm, that's interesting." You've got to go into these pages saying, "I'm going to shake myself up. I am not only willing to do better, I am committed to do better. I will try new ways of thinking, behaving, and feeling."

If you want to be outstanding—no matter what it is you want to do—then you're first going to have to stand up for you. You may find that the person who is truly holding you back is not a parent, or a teacher, or the world in general. What's holding you back is you. These Life Laws that you're about to learn will not only keep you standing, they'll get you moving forward so fast that it will make everyone else look like they're moving backward. But I repeat, it's your decision to stand up. It's up to you to take that initial risk and to stop being so fixed and rigid in the way you think, feel, and behave.

Change in your life can come slowly, but so what? What you'll realize is that the simple small improvements are what's going to transform your life forever. To get started on that journey, all you have to be is willing to try.

What's it going to hurt for you to make changes? You really want to make improvements in your life— then you should at least be open to moving your position.

BEFORE   AFTER

But I bet you, however, that once you learn the Life Laws, you'll never want to go back to the old you. So let's get to it!

LIFE LAW ONE

YOU EITHER GET IT, OR YOU DON'T

I think there is a world market for maybe five computers.

—Thomas Watson, Chairman of IBM (1943)

WHY YOU SHOULD READ THIS LIFE LAW:

To discover and use the huge power you have to change your life. Learn how the game is played so you can get unstuck and have more of what you want and need. Stop being pissed off and start winning. Become one who gets it.

KIM, A FRIEND OF MINE IN HIGH SCHOOL, HATED our cafeteria food, and at least once a week she would sneak off campus and go to one of the nearby fast-food places. The problem was that our principal caught her every time she came back and gave her a detention.

Kim hated detention but always thought she would get away with leaving "this time." She never did. By Christmas break Kim had served twenty-one detentions.

WHY IS THAT?

Next time your math teacher is droning on and on, why don't you let your mind wander a bit. Think about this: Why do some people seem to do so well while others, like Kim, seem lost and confused and don't appear to have a clue how to do any better?

Take it a step further. How is it, for instance, that Tom and Dave can score the same on an IQ test, yet Tom is a total waste at school while Dave makes straight As? Why is it that Meghan can maintain a great relationship with a guy while Laura, who's much better looking and more vivacious than Meghan, can't get a guy to take her out for more than two weeks? Why is it that Robert has been able to rise up from his abusive childhood and Amy has been able to succeed despite growing up poor while William, who comes from one of the most prominent and richest families in the city, is a total loser?

Why is it that the most popular girl in school is, in fact, the most popular girl in school? Why is it that the star athlete is so determined to succeed? Why is it that the school's class president is so good at organizing and presenting information? Why is it that some kids are so good-natured and so friendly you always want to sit with them at lunch?

Is it because they are more gifted than you? They've got genes that you don't?

Get real. Not a chance.

I hate to be blunt, but there's no better way to say this: These are people who have pulled their heads out of the clouds and decided to learn how the world works. They have stopped stumbling along, they have eliminated the types of behavior that just don't benefit them in the long run, and they have figured out what it's going to take to get the results they want. They don't stew over their problems, they don't look for excuses about why they can't get things done, and they don't get angry and pout about how life can be so unfair. Instead, they have made the effort to change their lives by accumulating certain information, putting together a plan, and applying the right skills.

In short, they "get it." They know that it isn't the luck of the draw that determines who gets to be successful. They know there isn't much guesswork involved in getting the results that matter— whether those results be good grades, starring roles in anything from a sports team to the drama club, more freedom and independence after school, or even happiness and a deeper sense of peace.

They know there is a kind of "system," or process, that can be used to get ahead of the pack. They have taken the time to study that system. For them, learning that system is no different than learning to drive a car or fly an airplane. They know there is work required to learn how to navigate through life. For them it's never been enough just to become aware that there is a system. They learn how to make that system work for them.

It's no different for you. All you have to do is learn that system and then work it, and you, too, will get what you want.

Sounds sort of cut-and-dried, doesn't it? All you have to do is follow a few rules. Learn a "system." You're thinking, "Come on, Jay, you don't know what you're talking about. Life is very anxiety-ridden, full of problems and weirdness, crazy parents, backstabbing friends, bossy teachers. How can that be?"

Trust me, all you have to do is work the system.

WORKING THE SYSTEM

Are you wondering just what in the heck I am talking about? Think back on the other people you know who are successful. The reason they "get it" is because they refuse to choose behaviors that they know will put them at a disadvantage with the rules of the world. What they do choose are behaviors that they know will get them the things that they want.

Here's an example of how the system works.

Grades: The guys and girls who "get it" in this world know that if they make poor grades, they get a poor level of respect. They know that if they make mediocre grades, they get only mediocre respect. They know that good grades create a level of respect and trust from parents and teachers that they cannot get any other way. They know that good grades lead to more freedom and more responsibility in life.

Here's the important thing: Those who "get it" know that the world's response to good grades is a fact of life that just isn't going to change. They accept that fact and they utilize it. When I was cruising (or so I thought) through my teens, I hopelessly did not "get it" about grades. Whenever the report card came out every six weeks my dad would sit me down for the big talk. He'd say, over and over, "How can you not want to study? How do you not have a thirst for knowledge? How can you not discipline yourself to do this? Don't you hate showing up at school and everybody thinks you're the guy who knows nothing?"

I think I heard the "thirst-for-knowledge" speech a thousand times. I'd tell my dad that I would really do better and study harder the next six weeks. But as soon as I was back in my room, I'd go back to staring at the ceiling. Apparently, I just didn't want to work the system. I'd rather have fun with my friends, concentrate on things like basketball—you know the story.

But did my refusal to work the system make me any happier? Was I more fulfilled living the carefree existence because I wasn't studying? I'm afraid not. I was always feeling slightly guilty, and slightly worried. Thank God I finally had my moment of epiphany, where I woke up and realized, "Hey, you male bimbo, who are you kidding here? This is your future that you're letting slip away from you." But if I had just "gotten it" when I was fifteen, my life would have been so much better, so much calmer, so much more rewarding.

Many of you are probably like me. You haven't spent much time learning and working the system. Some of you have just drifted along, thinking you can't really affect your destiny until you become an adult. Others of you are out there saying things like you shouldn't have to be judged on such things as your grades. You're saying, "I don't have to conform to the ways of the world."

Maybe you're right, but you're missing the point entirely. I'm not talking about right or wrong; I'm just talking about getting the results you want in your life, period. When you are one of those who "gets it," it's as if you are the star in the movie of your own life, and you are making things happen, rather than waiting for them to happen. You write your own script, you choose who is in the film, and you even direct the action that leads you to the ending you want. Instead of just reacting to whatever comes along in life, you get to live a life you have designed.

Sounds pretty fancy, but think about it. To get anywhere in life, to achieve any of your goals (even the most nonconformist ones), you have to figure out the best way to do it, and that requires you to figure out the rules you must follow and the roles you must play. You want to be a sports star in school? There is a system you have to work to get there. You want to be the most popular kid in school? There is a system you have to work to get there. You want to be in the chess club? There is a system you have to work to get there. You want to live with some passion in your life? There is a system you have to work to get there.

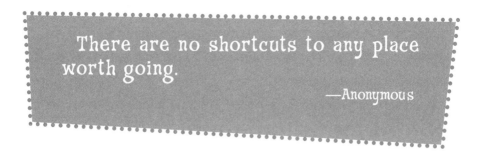

There are no shortcuts to any place worth going.

—Anonymous

THOSE WHO DON'T GET IT

Please understand, this is not a Life Law aimed only at those of you who want to be the super-great performers. It's also for all of you who know, deep down, that the time has come to put your life together. It's a Life Law for those of you who know you "should" do something about your life and who'd like to change, but who just aren't sure how to change. It's for those of you who blame circumstances for your place in life, but who don't know exactly how to find the circumstances you want. It's for those of you who feel so bored that you don't even like hanging out with yourself.

Think about how much time you've put into some aspects of your life. You've spent hours mastering video games, or sports, or memorizing songs. But you spend little or no time learning the system of life and then working it.

I'm not saying that your goal should be to become fanatically driven and so determined to be successful that you sacrifice all the other parts of your life. I'm not saying that at all. But there's a big difference between just going from day to day barely getting by, versus understanding who you are, how your life works, and how you can take the initiative to design your life. It's only when you finally "get it" that you can beat back all those lingering feelings of anxiety and confusion that you often have at night when you're sitting up in your bedroom alone wondering why no one seems to understand you. It's only when you finally "get it" that you can get to a place where you are no longer ignored, unfairly targeted, or flat-out run over. We know how easy it is for that to happen.

Think of what "getting it" will do for you. If you're in the game of life, whether you're currently playing the game at school for grades, or socially for popularity, or trying to land a certain girlfriend or boyfriend, or competing for a part-time after-school job, think of the incredible edge you will have over everybody else if you understand how the game works.

You will have an advantage because knowledge is definitely power. I see it all the time when I sucker my dad into playing video games with me. He doesn't have a clue how to score, he doesn't know where the trap doors are, he doesn't know how to generate extra points—so he fumbles along with a ham-fisted approach to a game he just doesn't understand. I slaughter him every single time. I don't mean some of the time; I mean every time. My dad is as smart as me and as quick as me and even has eyes as good as I do, but he just doesn't get it. Half the time he's holding the controller upside down.

No matter how highly you think of yourself, if you don't understand the rules of this world, you are not even a threat when you find yourself in competition with those who do get it, those who have the skills and know the rules. Let me tell you:

★ It's not uncool to know how the world works and to know how to get the things that you want.

★ It's not uncool to figure out a way to get along with your parents.

★ It's not uncool to find a way to get along with your teachers.

★ It's not uncool to say "No, that bothers me," when talking about behavior you don't want or you're not ready for, like drugs, alcohol, or sex.

★ It's not uncool to have a diversity of friends.

★ It's not uncool to get excited about something in your life, to find a passion, and to live with passion.

GETTING IT WITH OTHER PEOPLE

One of the best things about those who get it is that they realize that they have to interact with others. I know a lot of you believe that you can make your own way, march to your own drummer, and set your own agenda. Fine. You still have to interact with other people, and if you want to get anywhere at all, you must understand people, if for no other reason, so that you can get them to do what you want them to do. When you "get it" about other people—when you realize what drives their behavior—then you can use this knowledge for yourself and your own strategy to be successful.

Let me tell you about something that happened to my dad. This story taught me a lot about "getting it." Here's how he tells it:

> When I was in high school in Kansas City, I worked the night shift down at Hallmark Cards. When you get off work at two or three o'clock in the morning, it's a different world than what people see during the day. We were night owls looking for trouble, and we usually found some. A buddy of mine, who also worked at the plant, owned a Chevy Chevelle muscle car with over four hundred horsepower. After work, we liked to race around the deserted streets at ridiculous speeds, looking for a drag race with some other late-night moron with a hundred dollars to bet.
>
> One night, during the Christmas holiday, we had two passengers on our late-night prowls: a longtime friend visiting me from a small town, and a friend of the driver's whom I had not met before. Under my then-theory that stupidity was a virtue, we were doing well over a hundred miles an hour on Main

Street, right on the fringe of downtown Kansas City, when an unmarked patrol car appeared out of nowhere, clinging to our bumper. His car was apparently pretty fast, too. He didn't seem to want to race; I was pretty sure he didn't have any beer to share, and boy, did he look mad.

Skipping the usual practice of flooding us with spotlights and calling for backup, the patrolman pulled us over and leaped out of his car, slamming his door so hard we could feel it. I don't know if this cop was truly a giant or just looked that way that night, but he looked big enough to have his own weather systems, and it definitely looked like a storm was brewing.

As the officer stomped up to the car, my buddy's friend panicked. Wriggling and sliding out the rear window, he dropped headfirst to the sidewalk and took off running. If that cop wasn't mad enough before, he was now. It was bad enough that we had violated his turf; now, because one of us had run away, we had further insulted him and defied his authority.

The policeman yanked the driver's door open, grabbed my buddy by the collar, dragged him out, and ordered us to follow suit. Holding my friend by the collar, he said, "I'm going to ask you one @!&Z$ time: Who is that boy that ran off?"

In his most surly and sarcastic tone, my buddy snarled, "Well, his name is . . . Sam Sausage! What of it?" I remember thinking,

"Buddy, you just don't get it." That cop hit him so hard it almost broke *my* nose.

Up to that point, I had been worried about getting a ticket or an impounded car. Given the turn of events, that would have been a godsend. Apparently, this particular officer was not real big on paperwork. My small-town friend was, unfortunately for him, next in line. His problem was, he really didn't know the runner's name, and neither did I, so my prospects were not looking too good, either. Now the cop ran the same drill. Grabbing the collar of my friend (who was now wishing he could "beam" back to "Nowhere, USA"), he looked him in the eye and said, "I'm gonna ask you one @!&Z$ time: Who is that boy that ran off?"

Well, as I said, my friend may not have known his name, but he did know what probably wasn't going to be the best answer. With absolutely no surliness and no attitude, and with all the sincerity that a petrified, cottonmouthed kid could muster, he said, "Sir, I swear to you on my mother's grave (she was of course alive and well back in "Nowhere"), I don't know his name, but, sir, I can promise you this: I am absolutely certain it is not Sam Sausage."

As scared as I was, I instantly thought, "Now he gets it. We may live through this yet." I said not a word, figuring this cop needed a really good leaving alone. My dad had taught me there are times in life when you just don't want to miss a good chance to *shut up*. This was clearly one of those times. One guy did not get it, and he was kissing the pavement and would sport two black eyes for the next several weeks. One guy did get it, and he was still vertical and could see out of both of his eyes. A stark contrast. I can assure you that we never traveled over twenty-five miles an hour on that cop's beat again, ever. Life just goes better when you are one of those who gets it.

Now to avoid "kissing the pavement" yourself, you have to be willing to learn the Life Laws and how things work so that you can fold all of that into your life.

WHAT MAKES EVERYONE TICK

To give you a running start in building a strategy for the way you deal with others, I want to share with you some of the most common characteristics of all people. If you understand these common things it can help you know how to deal with people and be more effective.

I'm no Dave Letterman, but let me give you my Top 10 list straight from Dorm 66 at the University of Texas. This Top 10 list is made up of things that are almost always present in all people. If you know these things, you have a great understanding about your teachers, friends, parents, brothers and sisters, and anyone else you encounter in your life. Already, right now, when you finish reading this list, you will know things that 99.9 percent of the people in the world don't know. Here are the ten most significant common characteristics:

TOP 10 LIST FROM DORM 66 AT THE UNIVERSITY OF TEXAS

10. Even when it's not Halloween, everybody wears a mask. You must look beyond the mask to see the person.

9. Even good people have bad days.

8. People often do things for other than the apparent reasons.

7. People like, trust, and believe those who like them.

6. People hear only what they understand.

5. Everybody prefers to talk about things that are important to him or her.

4. Everybody, including my sweet old Grandma Jerry, approaches every situation with at least some concern about. "What's in it for me?"

3. People are easier to manage if you are friendly instead of bossy.

2. Everyone's number-one need is acceptance.

1. Everyone's number-one fear is rejection.

Think about why knowing just these ten things about people can start moving you in the direction of becoming one of those who gets it. Take trait four: Everybody approaches every situation with at least some concern about "what's in it for me?" If you come to appreciate that, then you are going to understand that if you want to persuade someone to do something, to think a certain way, or allow you to do a certain thing, you are going to have to figure out some way that there is something in it for them.

You may be surprised to hear me say that I believe all people are selfish. But I am just telling you how it is. I am just saying that if you understand these characteristics about the way we all act—and if you understand the universal needs of another human being—then you know how to make things happen. To ignore these "givens" about people would be the same as sealing your fate before you even begin. Failure is not an accident. You either set yourself up for it or you don't.

ARE YOU READY TO GET IT?

If you stay focused, and if you start applying the rest of the Life Laws, you will "get it." You will set yourself up for success.

You do not have to be the brightest person in the crowd, but you do have to be eager and tenacious. You have to decide that you will become one who gets it no matter what. You have to develop a quality of pushing through when the going is tough. You get it by working and trying harder, inch by inch.

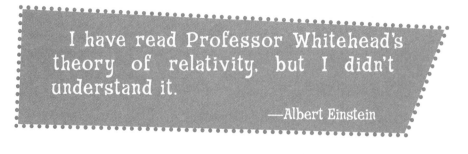

I have read Professor Whitehead's theory of relativity, but I didn't understand it.

—Albert Einstein

You also must resolve to find out how you work from the inside out. I am talking here about making yourself a project. You have other projects at school, at home, or at your church or temple. What I want you to do is make yourself a project.

If you want to "get it," then it's time for you to begin. You become the jump start for altering your life and increasing its quality. I want to stress that these are learned skills. This is knowledge that must be acquired. Maya Angelou has eloquently said, "You did what you knew how to do, and when you knew better, you did better." This and the next nine Life Laws will help you know better so that you can do better.

Congratulations! Whether you know it or not, you are already moving into the driver's seat of life. You are already setting the wheels of change into motion, which is one of the hardest parts of the process.

Now let's get you up to speed.

LIGHTBULBS

- You can choose to be one who "gets it."

- The world works as a system; if you learn that system you will have an advantage over everybody else.

- It is not uncool to want a better life and work toward getting it.

- Learning and using the Life Laws will help you become one who "gets it."

LIFE LAW TWO

YOU CREATE YOUR OWN EXPERIENCE

This life is worth living, we can say, since it is what we make it.

—William James

WHY YOU SHOULD READ THIS LIFE LAW:

To solve the mystery of why your role in this life is what it is. Get the tools to set it up differently by changing the statement you make to the world in everything wyou do.

TONY WAS BIGGER AND STRONGER THAN MOST people in our class, and he loved acting macho. He wouldn't just walk up to a group. He'd flex and pose as he came toward you, then he'd grab you and brag about how strong and tough he was. He obviously did this because it was the one thing that he felt distinguished himself in a crowd. He thought it impressed people, when in fact, everyone just rolled their eyes and mimicked him behind his back.

Lindsey was just as bad. When you would talk with her she was incredibly nice, but it didn't take long to realize that she was the world's worst gossip. She wouldn't just pass on the truth, she would make stuff up as she went along. She was horrible, and two weeks into the year, nobody would even come near her.

Why, instead of growing in popularity, did Tony and Lindsey each become more and more of a loser? Because they refused to pay attention to the way they created their own experience. Or to put it another way, they did nothing to change the way people experienced them.

I'm using obvious examples to make a point. The point is that you control the way the world responds to you by the way you conduct yourself. When I talk about you creating your own experience, I'm talking about the statement you make to the world through your attitude and appearance and the world's response to you. As you progress in this book and start to formulate your strategy for a better life, you have to keep asking yourself how you are currently creating your own experience. Have you created your experience in a way that works for you? Or does it not work for you?

IF YOU LOOK AND ACT LIKE A DUMB-ASS, YOU WILL BE TREATED LIKE ONE

What you're about to learn is that your entire experience in the world is determined solely by how you engage the world. The way everyone reacts to you—from friends to parents to strangers—is due to the way you present yourself. It's due to the way you create your self-image.

The good news is that you decide which role you want to play, and thus you decide which response you want to receive from the world. You decide because you choose the behaviors that put you in each of these roles.

You choose:

* **How you dress**
* **How you talk**
* **What kind of friends you have**
* **Who you date**
* **Where you hang out**
* **Whether or not you respect your elders**
* **Whether or not you break the law**
* **Whether or not you do drugs or drink**
* **What kind of friend you are**
* **What kind of work ethic you have**
* **Whether your word is good or not**
* **Whether you are a giver or a taker**

As you can see, you choose your behavior. I'm not trying to preach to you and tell you that you should or shouldn't dress a certain way or you should or shouldn't do drugs. All I am saying is that you must be responsible for the reaction that comes with your choice. If you're a loner, it's because you set it up that way. If you're in constant conflict with authority, it's because you set it up that way. If you don't like the way everybody is reacting to you, you set it up that way by the way you engage the world. The good news is that you can choose to change that. You can choose to act differently and present yourself differently, and you will get a different response.

If you don't like something, change it. If you can't change it, change your attitude. Don't complain.

—Maya Angelou

THE ROLES WE PLAY

Here's the most important question for you to answer: What is the "role" you tend to play when you engage the world?

All of us play some sort of "role"—some of us are jocks or drama mamas, others of us are brainiacs. Some of us play the Goth role, all dressed in black, and others of us play the preppie role, all dressed in Abercrombie & Fitch. The role we play sends out a message. It teaches people to respond to you a certain way. As unfortunate and unfair as it is, people will often stereotype you, placing you in a certain role, and thus they will always have a fixed response to you.

As you go through this chapter, I want you to start asking yourself some questions about what role you play and how that is creating your experience. Here are some to begin with:

1. Stand at a mirror and study your clothes, your hair, and your posture. What do you think your appearance—your "look"—is saying to others?

2. Think about the way you meet strangers. How do you speak to them? What do you think is the initial impression you make on them?

3. How do you talk to your parents? Do you make rebellious statements? Or are you a willing spirit?

4. What is your personality like around other students? Are you a giver or a taker? Are you warm or distant?

What kind of integrity do you think you convey to others? Are you sincere, or are you a gossip? Are you a good friend, or are you a back-stabber?

With that information in hand, it's time for you to take a good look at the roles you play in life and decide if those roles are getting you the treatment that you want. Listed below are many of the roles that you probably see at your school; do you see yourself in any of them? Is the experience that you're creating working for you, allowing you to engage the world with honesty and integrity? Or are you operating off the worst parts of yourself, hiding your true feelings with false roles? Are you using your roles to share yourself fully or are you using your roles to protect yourself from potential hurt?

Goody-two-shoes

You just want to tell these people to give it a rest. They have to do everything more than right, and in doing so, make everybody else look like a slacker. (Don't confuse a goody-two-shoes with someone who is genuinely moral.)

★ They are always five minutes early for class and never forget their homework.

★ They bring clean folded gym clothes every day of the week.

Prom Queen

This girl is the social butterfly. In her eyes, life is nothing but a popularity contest.

★ Everybody is her best friend when she needs something.

★ She is as artificial as NutraSweet.

Tease

This girl flirts with every guy in school but squirms at the thought of even holding hands.

★ Look for these girls hanging out about halfway to first base.

★ This girl's goal in life is to lead people on.

Jock

For these people, class is just a time to rest up for their next game.

* Jocks don't have friends; they only have teammates.
* If you see them carrying books, I'll bet you they are just play-books.

The Whiner

These people are always complaining about something, and it is never their fault.

* They make country music sound peppy.
* They always think they are the victim.

Drama Mama

You thought only *ER* was tragic. Nothing—and I mean nothing—is ordinary to these people.

* Everything is always the best or worst, or the nicest or meanest thing that has ever been done.
* Everything they say is discounted as exaggeration.

Teacher's Pet

This is the moron who ruins your opportunity to leave class five minutes early by asking ten minutes of questions about nothing.

* They always sit in the front row for class and can be found clapping chalkboard erasers after class.
* They never miss an opportunity to raise their hand.

Gossip

These people are absolutely insufferable. They always have some information, usually misinformation, about something. Never trust them, because if they will do it with you, they will do it to you.

*   **They are always whispering to someone (their new best friend).**
*   **Most, if not all, of the things they say are either made up or highly sensationalized stories about others.**

Slacker

Don't look for these people in the library. Unless a remote control and a bag of potato chips are involved, the slacker is not interested.

*   **A slacker's best role model is Bart Simpson.**
*   **Alarm clock? No way!**

Perfecto

These people invented the locker organizer. With them, everything has to be in perfect order.

*   **Something is always wrong in these people's lives.**
*   **When they make a 99 on a test, they will fight for two days for that last point. Enough already.**

Druggies

You will find these people in the lunchroom at lunchtime with the munchies, if you know what I mean. They are always thinking about getting high.

   ★   **These people know more about side effects than a pharmacist.**

   ★   **Keep in mind, "a dime" carries a whole other meaning with these people!**

Granola

These people look like they have been on "Survivor Island" all semester. They would wear a potato sack if it met the school dress code.

   ★   **They own no shampoo and use even less soap.**

   ★   **Their wardrobe is as boring as economics class.**

The Glamour-puss

This is the girl who comes to school with the four-hour hairdo looking like she put her makeup on with a paintbrush. Everything, and I do mean everything—hair, makeup, and clothes—has to be absolutely perfect at all times. If the building is on fire, her only concern is how she looks in that lighting.

   ★   **What you see is all you get.**

   ★   **You can identify a glamour-puss because she is posing for an imaginary cameraman.**

Brainiacs

These are the people who are so smart they will read *The Odyssey* in Greek, just in case something was lost in the translation.

★ Unlike Perfecto, they make 100 on the test.

★ The idea of a relaxing weekend to these guys is to just do some advanced trigonometry.

Greasers

These guys would rather work on their cars than drive them; but never forget, they don't have cars, they have hot rods. The glamour-puss and prom queen frequently use the greaser's hood for a mirror.

★ When you talk to these guys it is like speaking another language. They list car parts like doctors list body parts.

★ If they ever do let you in their hot rod, they will make you take your shoes off before you get in.

Pig Pens

I have met horses that smell better than these people. They are just flat-out filthy.

★ They will use their pencil lead to get the dirt out from under their fingernails in class.

★ These guys' idea of art is their booger collection on their bedroom wall.

Minions

Minions will never say no. They are always doing what someone else says they should do.

* **A minion will never ever have an original thought.**
* **Minions are constantly doing something for somebody else.**

Marilyn Mansons

These people are always dressed for a funeral, even when nobody has died.

* **These guys don't buy necklaces, they buy collars.**
* **Come on, guys, lose the black nail polish.**

TAKING ACCOUNTABILITY FOR YOUR LIFE

I probably don't have to tell you that if you stay stuck in these roles, pretending to be something you are not, you are creating an experience for yourself that is never going to provide any real success. And it's easy—real easy—to get stuck in those roles. The question is whether the roles you are choosing are creating the experience you really want out of life.

Let me tell you what happened to me when I was sixteen years old. I was the starting point guard for my high school basketball team, the Greenhill Hornets, and I felt on top of the world. It was early December, and we were on our way to what many predicted was a championship season. Parents and classmates poured into the stands to watch us. My heart pounded with pride each time my name was called during the player introductions prior to the game.

We were invited to a mid-season tournament consisting of all the powerhouses of the city, and I was pumped. As I took the court for that

first game, I was hit with a wave of excitement. We were going to win; I could just feel it. Then thirty seconds into the tournament, I passed the ball to the wing, broke to the basket, and got an instantaneous pass back. I drove left and had my man beat. I planted my left foot to cut behind him . . . and it happened. My life changed in less than a second. I lay screaming in a heap on the floor, screaming in pain and holding my knee as my foot flopped from one side to the other.

All I wanted at that point was for someone to hold my foot still so maybe the pain would stop. But the pain wouldn't stop. My dad and my coach had to help me off the court and into the locker room. For me, the game was over, the tournament was over, the season was over. It was surreal that I could be driving the lane one minute and being driven to the hospital the next.

The doctor on call gave me one quick look; no exam was necessary. Not wanting to be the one who told me, he pulled my dad aside, but I could still hear the doctor talking under his breath. Pain still on fire in my leg, I made out seven words that hurt nearly as much as the injury itself, ". . . it's bad, he may not play again . . ."

And it was bad. I had torn ligaments in my knee and couldn't even walk without crutches. I spent two weeks in a funk, because this was a huge deal to me. Everybody has one thing that defines them in life, and for me, my passion was basketball. Being a basketball player was something I had been working for since the fifth grade, attending summer basketball camps, playing in YMCA leagues, working endless hours on my fundamentals in the driveway with my dad. This was the experience I had created for myself, the role I had carved out in my school and in life. When I made the high school varsity basketball team, I was living my dream, and in a split second, it was gone. I couldn't believe life had dealt me such a blow. It was so unfair, so cruel. I would limp around school, grimacing as I moved from classroom to classroom on my crutches, always glancing up to make sure that people were giving me the proper, sympathetic looks.

After my injury I created a new experience for myself. I began to play the role of the whiner. It was an easy role to take on, in large part because it kept me from having to deal with a huge question that lay in front of me: "So who are you going to be now?"

"You know," my dad finally said, "no one's going to feel sorry for you for very long. I absolutely hate what's happened to you. But that doesn't change the fact that you are going to have to create a new role, a new plan, and get yourself back up and going again."

"Oh, no," I thought. I looked for the nearest door. This was not the time to hear another speech from the Old Man.

"I'm not asking anyone to feel sorry for me," I said defensively.

"Sure you are," he said. "Look at you. You wake up every day making sighs and doing the poor-pitiful-me act. How long do you think it's going to work?"

"What are you talking about?"

"Jay, what are you accomplishing having people feel sorry for you? How are you helping yourself by getting on the phone every night and

telling your friends how fate dealt you a bad hand the other night at a basketball game? Have you noticed the coach has already got another player to take your place?"

Man, was he bugging me with all that accountability crap! "Hey," I said, "can't I be disappointed that my knee is totally screwed up?"

"Yes, but that doesn't mean that you can't do anything about it. You might not be able to control everything that happens to you, but you can control what you do about it."

"Here we go," I thought.

"How about coming up with a strategy to rehabilitate your leg so you can get in a position to walk again and then maybe play basketball again?" Dad asked.

"A strategy?" This wasn't a chess game we were talking about.

"I haven't seen any sign that you're doing a thing except bitching and moaning," he said.

Do you know that feeling you get when a parent makes you mad? That feeling that you want to pack up all your stuff and move to India?

Meanwhile, Dad kept bearing in. "How long do you want to play this role—the role of the whiner?"

I was furious at him for the way he was jacking with me. But whining wasn't getting me back in shape, so I decided I would formulate a strategy. I got on a stationary bicycle and began pedaling it backward at about one mile an hour because I didn't have enough strength to go forward. I did it for weeks, feeling as if no progress was being made whatsoever. I did it as the basketball team finished its season. I did it without any applause. I did it without any cheers from the crowd. I did it just for me because I knew that I was the only one who cared. Nobody else even knew how miserable I was.

> Press on. Nothing in the world can take the place of persistence.
> —Ray A. Kroc (founder of McDonald's)

But you know what? Once that commitment began—once I started holding myself accountable—my circumstances did change. After several weeks, I was able to pedal forward on the bicycle. Then I was able to walk without a limp. I stuck with the program, and before long, I was able to lift weights. That enabled me to jog and run. Then two weeks before I was supposed to even look at a basketball, I sneaked out to my backyard, and while no one was looking, I picked up my basketball and took that layup I was going for when I blew out my knee the first time. I was back. It had all paid off, and before too long, I was on the basketball court shooting hoops with my friends. Finally, the next season rolled around, and on a late autumn afternoon, less than a year after my knee injury, my name was called on the public address system as Greenhill's starting guard.

Because of what I did, I didn't get my name in *Sports Illustrated*. I didn't get a medal, I didn't get a certificate, I didn't even get a cookie. No news crews showed up for my return. In fact, as far as the big picture of my life goes, my high school basketball career means very little. But what will always remain important for me about all of this is that I realized I did not have to let a certain set of circumstances control me. I was able to come back from what I perceived at the time was a disastrous situation and create the circumstances to make me feel good about myself again. I had the option of sitting on the couch complaining, which would make me no happier, or going out and doing something about my problem. So I went out and created a better circumstance for myself.

Those small steps, which at the beginning of my commitment seemed light-years from full-contact basketball, accumulated into meaningful results. I could have laid around and made a decision to complain about the circumstances I found myself in. I could have said that I was a victim of a bad experience. But instead, I went out and created a new experience for myself.

You can do the same thing. You can do it right now by taking small steps. If you're sitting at home with a hundred pounds to lose, or a D average, or a bad relationship with your parents, you can start taking steps out of those situations.

Understand, though, that whether you like it or not, you are creating your own experience. The only choice you have is whether you create a good experience or a bad experience.

LIGHTBULBS

- You choose the statement you make to the world with your attitude and appearance. When you choose that statement, you choose how the world will respond to you.

- If you don't like the way people treat you, you can change that by changing the statement you make to them.

- What role do you play? Is it getting you the results that you want?

- You, and you alone, are responsible for the experiences you have in life.

LIFE LAW THREE

PEOPLE DO WHAT WORKS

All men should strive to learn before they die what they are running from, and to, and why.

—James Thurber

WHY YOU SHOULD READ THIS LIFE LAW:

To find out where you have become addicted to hidden payoffs that suck you into self-destructive and self-defeating things. Find out what they are and how to break their grip. Learn to work for the healthy payoffs.

Let's see if you've been in one of these situations:

YOU DO SOMETHING REALLY STUPID OVER AND over. Maybe what you do is spend your night watching television instead of studying for tests that you have to take the next day, even though you know that you need to make good grades on those tests to keep your grade-point average high enough to get into college the next year.

Or maybe you sneak out of the house and go to parties where you drink alcohol, even though your parents have warned you many times that if you are caught doing such a thing, you would not be allowed to go on a summer vacation that you are dying to go on. As you sneak back into the house after one of those parties, the lights come on. There stand your parents. You are busted.

Or maybe you come in from a long day of school, and your little sister has been waiting all day long for you because she thinks you hung the moon. But instead of showing any affection, you blast your little sister. "Get away from me. Don't touch my stuff in my room. Get out of here. I hate you bugging me." Then you slam the door in her face as you have many times before, and she races off crying to your parents.

Now, in these kinds of situations, what inevitably happens next? That's right. One of your parents sits you down, gets right in your face, and says, "What were you thinking?"

"I don't know," you reply, hanging your head.

"So why did you do what you just did?"

And what do you always say in these situations? "Uh, I don't know."

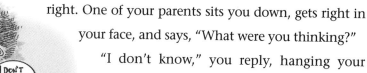

DO YOU REALLY NOT KNOW?

Do you ever wonder if you are some kind of oddball because you behave in ways that make no sense at all? Do you ever feel really guilty because you do things that you know without a doubt could get you in serious trouble, yet you just can't seem to stop doing them? Do you feel horrible because you do things that you know hurt other people, but you still do them over and over?

I don't have to tell you that there are some behaviors we repeat—a pattern of behaviors—that just don't make sense. You get drunk even when you know the consequences of getting caught. You don't study even when you know the consequences of an F. You get involved in sexual situations with someone even though you know the consequences of going too far. Even though you say to yourself it only makes things worse when you scream at your parents, you still find yourself screaming at your parents. Even though you say you're going to spend a weekend getting a lot of stuff done that you've been putting off (cleaning your room, visiting your grandmother, etc.), you end up sitting around on Saturday and Sunday.

> Hold yourself responsible for a higher standard than anybody expects of you. Never excuse yourself.
>
> —Henry Ward Beecher

Then you say to yourself or to your parents such statements as, "I don't know why I do that," or "I don't mean to do that," or "I don't want to do that."

But the truth is that you *do* want to do it or you wouldn't repeat the behavior. You absolutely want to do it. You are not weird, you are not crazy, and you are certainly not stupid. You are just not aware that there is a powerful set of influences that's got you by the throat. These influences, which are largely unconscious, are leading you to repeat behaviors that are ultimately damaging to your life.

You might consciously say to yourself that you don't like the behavior. You don't like the idea of you being a drug user, or you don't like the idea of you being sexually promiscuous, or you don't like the idea of you being sullen and rebellious around teachers and parents. You don't like the image of yourself as irresponsible, or lazy, or even dangerous. But at an unconscious level, these behaviors are giving you something that you want very much. They're giving you some sort of quick fix—an immediate reward. They're giving you a "payoff."

Are you confused? All right, follow this. No one would dispute the fact that we repeat certain behaviors because the results are satisfying to us in some way. For instance, you go out and run three mornings a week and lose ten pounds, or you lift weights three times a week and build lots of muscle. Because you get a great reward for exercising, you keep doing it. The behavior works for you. Conversely, if you do not repeat a behavior, then it's because the result is not desirable. If you think about it, this is not some off-the-wall concept. When you touch a hot stove, the result is undesirable. You burn the heck out of your hand. So—hey, huge insight coming here!—you don't repeat that behavior because this behavior does not work for you.

So far, so good, right? Then, obviously, if we are repeating behaviors that we consciously say are not good for us—smoking cigarettes, or fighting with your brother, for instance—then the payoffs from those behaviors are in some way working for us. It doesn't matter if we know that the long-term consequences of these behaviors aren't good for us. We like the immediate reward that comes from these payoffs. Even though at a conscious level we despise the behavior, at a different level we *are* getting something out of it. The payoff may be subtle and it may be unhealthy; but it *is* there. You are not an exception because there is no exception.

Now here's why all this information is important for you to know. If you want to start taking real control over your life and start making better decisions instead of repeating behavior that you already know is not good for you—behavior that ultimately ruins your self-esteem and threatens your safety—then you've got to figure out what these "influences" are that are making you screw up so badly. It's not good enough to say, "Oh, I wish I didn't do that" or "I wish I wasn't that way." You have to connect the dots between your self-defeating behavior and the payoff you are getting from that behavior.

Your job is to discover what is really going on inside you that makes you act angry, or rebellious, or self-destructive. If you can do that, then you are on your way to breaking that cycle of negative attitudes and behaviors that are holding you back. You will be able to get more control in your life and, most important, you'll be able to maintain that self-control. You probably won't slip and start returning to old behaviors and screwing up again.

Allow me to illustrate this. I asked a bunch of kids to identify things in their lives that they totally hated doing yet continued to do. Read these confessions and see if you can relate:

★ *John, age seventeen:* "My teachers think I'm one of the brightest kids at school. They always tell me I'm going places. And I know I will be successful—very successful . . . But there is one thing I do that can screw that up. Sometimes at the mall, I like to walk through the stores and look at the merchandise—like the smaller merchandise that can fit into my pocket. Like jewelry, stuff I could give a girl. I'm pretty good at slipping it into my pocket without anyone seeing. Then I'm gone. Yeah, I know what could happen if I got caught. I could get arrested and there goes a college scholarship. [He stops smiling and stares at the floor.] I always say I've got to stop. But yeah, yeah, I still do it."

★ *Andrew, age sixteen:* "Compared to other kids, I've got a pretty great relationship with my parents. They've given me a car, given me late curfews, let me have backyard parties. I know I should always tell them more often how much I appreciate what they've done for me. But there will be times at dinner that Mom starts droning on and on about something boring that happened to her or one of her friends, and I just lose it. I start getting mad. I tell her stuff like, 'Mom, can you be more boring?' She gets upset, and I can tell I hurt her; I hate that, but sometimes I can't help it."

★ *Laura, age fifteen:* "I'm a high school sophomore, and sometimes I get invited over to parties where I know a bunch of senior guys are going to be. I don't know what to think about them. They're always flirting with me in a strange way. They brush up against my body when they pass by in the hallways. They always tell me that I shouldn't be the last virgin in high school. I don't like it. They sort of treat me like an object. I still go to their parties. [Long pause.] But I think I can handle it. I really do."

* *Larry, age eighteen:* "I know people around school think that I can sometimes be an asshole. I can be pretty rude. I'm pretty good at putting down people who I don't like. I could tone it down some, sure. Okay, there are some people who don't deserve the abuse I fire at them. But, well, it's just something I do. I don't want anybody to think they can walk over me."

* *Elyse, age sixteen:* "I guess I'm overweight by about thirty pounds. I used to be petite, but then I started eating too much and exercising too little—and all the weight caught up with me. I know I've got to get back to the way I used to look. It's what I really want to happen. Appearance is very important to me. I say that to myself every night, over and over. But at 10 P.M., it's like a bell goes off in my head, and I have to eat something. I usually end up eating a candy bar that I keep under my bed."

THE POWER OF A PAYOFF

Now, you might have read about these guys and said, "Hey, don't they get it? They're acting stupid!" But the chances are good that you're doing something similar yourself. You're doing it because of your need for the "payoff" that comes from that behavior. Whether you are able to

admit this or not, that payoff is a huge force in shaping who you are.

Let's talk for a moment about what a payoff is. It can take many different forms: physical, mental, social, psychological, and emotional.

For John, his payoff for shoplifting could very well be the adrenaline-like rush that comes with taking a risk. For Andrew, who yells at his mother, the payoff is that he gets to vent his frustration, to release some pent-up tension. Even though he later says he hates the way he treats his mother, he is creating those scenes on purpose so he can display anger. For Laura, the girl who goes to the parties, the payoff could be that she gets real intense attention from other guys. Even if she stays worried that she is putting herself into a potentially dangerous situation, the attention remains too intoxicating. For Larry, who's sometimes downright cruel with his criticisms of others, perhaps the payoff is that he gets to feel more secure by "getting" others before they "get" him. And for Elyse, who keeps eating even when she wants to stop, the payoff for that candy bar each night is not only that she finds some psychological comfort in food. It could be that she finds some psychological comfort in staying heavy. She gets a payoff for staying fat. Does that make any sense? Yes, because as long as she stays that way, she can tell herself she is not liked because she is fat. She feels safer if she stays heavy.

You know, I used to think my dad was a little nuts when he'd tell me that the reason I wasn't doing my homework was because I was getting a payoff for it. He'd say, "Jay, you wouldn't keep screwing up over and over about your grades if there wasn't some payoff you were getting for your screwups."

"What kind of BS is this?" I'd ask myself.

"The results you're getting from not doing your homework have to be desirable to some part of yourself. Otherwise, you wouldn't keep behaving that way all the time," he'd say.

"Dad, I do want to have good grades," I'd reply.

"No you don't. Otherwise, you'd do your homework."

"So then what is this so-called payoff I'm getting for not doing my homework?"

"That's for you to figure out."

"Well, I'm just a little lazy, that's all."

"No, you're not lazy," he'd say. "I've watched you get yourself back in shape for basketball all on your own. I've watched you work very hard at lots of things without me or someone else standing over you and cracking the whip."

One day after another of my dirtbag report cards, my dad came and asked me directly: "So what's your payoff for not doing your homework?"

"Dad, I've told you, I don't have a payoff. I just need to work harder."

"Once again, Jay, if there wasn't some kind of payoff, even an unconscious one, you would have started working harder a long time ago. So let me ask you. Could it be that you're a little scared about what might happen to you if you do your homework?"

"Scared?" I said, putting on as cynical a face as I could muster. "I'm not scared of anything."

Dad gave me that "Jay-you-are-such-a-dumb-ass" expression and said, "Maybe your payoff is that you don't have to admit to yourself what kind of potential you have. As long as you stay a C student, you get a payoff by not having to live with the responsibility of being a top performer."

I felt the steam rising up in me. I was angry. What made me most angry, of course, was that I didn't want to admit that he was, once again, right. I didn't want to be a top performer, because once I was, I would constantly be forced to live up to that expectation.

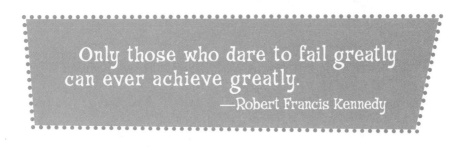

Only those who dare to fail greatly can ever achieve greatly.
—Robert Francis Kennedy

Now it's your turn. In just a moment we're going to do an exercise called "What is your payoff?" It's time for you to identify the behaviors that you know aren't working but that you can't seem to stop. Maybe your behavior that you don't like is that you experiment with drugs. If so, what is the payoff? Is it that you like the physical feeling of being high? Or maybe it's that you get to escape, however briefly, from a life that you think is pretty lousy? Maybe your payoff—and be honest here—is that drugs make you feel as if you belong to a group, even if that group is only a group of druggies who have no criteria for membership in their group except that you snort, smoke, or swallow the same thing they do?

Or let's say you smoke cigarettes. You know, of course, that you shouldn't smoke because you know what the consequences of smoking will be in the long run: death. But you smoke anyway, because you like the immediate results—the payoff. Smoking makes you feel in control, it makes you look more mature, it makes you look cool. For you, the potential penalty, lung cancer, seems so far off in the future that it's irrelevant.

How about this situation, which so many of us have had to face: alcohol. Let's say your parents give you a car, but with that car comes one very explicit warning. Your parents say that if they ever catch you drinking while driving, they'll immediately take the car away from you and sell it, and they promise you that you will be walking everywhere for the rest of your high school life. By anyone's standards, that's a pretty frightening consequence.

So what do you do? A Friday night comes along and your friends call and say, "Hey, let's go out cruising in your car." Someone brings along a couple of six-packs. There's a voice inside you saying, "Shut down this trip right now." But even though you know you'll lose your car for the rest of your high school years if you get caught, you put the car into gear, take off, and grab a beer.

Let's be honest. Whether to drink, or not to drink, is one of the big issues in your life. You love the immediate payoff that comes with drinking. You get to participate in an act that everyone says is fun, you don't miss anything that your friends are doing, and you feel sort of "cool" for taking a gamble. But then the next day comes around and you say, "What if my parents had caught me? What if I had gotten caught by the police and gotten arrested? What if I had been driving and hit a car and caused a wreck? I've got to stop this."

Then the next weekend comes around and, well—you know the rest of the story. You go out and do it again.

Don't just look at the payoffs that come from your most dramatic negative behavior. Some of your payoffs are coming from more subtle negative behavior. Look at this chart and see if you find yourself in here some way.

NEGATIVE BEHAVIOR	PAYOFF
Shyness	No risk of rejection if you reach out
Temper	Tension release
Sarcasm	Don't have to show true emotions
Mediocrity	No pressure to perform
Showing off	Get much-longed-for attention
Laziness	Don't have to get involved in life

Now that we know why we don't want to do things, let's talk about how to stop doing them.

WHAT IS YOUR PAYOFF?

In the space that follows, list five of the most frustrating and persistent negative behavioral patterns or situations in your life. These are patterns that are negative to you. Write down anything you do, or any way you act, that makes you later say, "I wish I hadn't been that way."

1. ....

2. ....

3. ....

4. ....

5. ....

Now, in the space below, write down what you think is your payoff for each of these behaviors.

1. ....

2. ....

3. ....

4. ....

5. ....

BLOCKING THE PAYOFF

Are you starting to connect the dots? The good news is that connecting the dots gives you a lot of power just by becoming aware of what you have been doing. Just by becoming aware of these payoffs, you'll be able to take a fresh look at yourself and start making more informed and, certainly, more mature decisions. Just by turning the spotlight on this part of yourself that you never look at, you'll also find that you won't be as susceptible to so many negative influences. It's like learning how a magic trick is done. When you know the "secret" to the magic trick, it loses its luster.

Let's return once again to John, Andrew, Laura, Larry, and Elyse. John now has figured out that he's got a thrill-seeking impulse. It's what has led him to shoplift. At this point, he can stand back, look at his life, and say, "Is there any other way I can get a thrill without doing something that could ruin my future? Maybe pick up a hobby like dirtbike riding?" You see, he's informed. He has gathered much more information about himself and his behavior and the consequences of that behavior.

How about Andrew, who yells at his mom? What Andrew has discovered is that his real source of frustration is with other students—a girlfriend who isn't treating him right, and a group of friends who don't include him the way he wants to be included. Yet it's difficult to lash out at them. If he lashes out at his girlfriend or his friends, he's afraid he'll push them away. So he finds a safe place to get out his anger: his mom, who isn't going to lash back at him. Now that he knows he's abusing his mother that way just for a payoff, hurting someone he loves very much, Andrew feels horrible for being so gutless, and for the first time, his behavior toward his mom starts to change.

When Laura understands that her deep need for attention from other guys is leading her into real trouble, then she starts figuring out more effective and safer ways to win proper attention from her friends. When Larry understands that his payoff for being so rude around his classmates is that he gets to hide from his own feelings of insecurity, then he starts to realize that the best way to find security is to reach out instead of rejecting others. When Elyse begins to figure out that

her fears about not being liked even if she becomes thin are really unfounded, she is finally willing to create a kind of lifestyle that lets her lose weight.

When you realize the negative nature of your payoff, you'll naturally protect yourself against it. When I understood, for instance, what my payoff really was for not studying, I found myself saying, "Wait a second. This is crap. I'm not going to let fear control me. I'm better than this. I don't want to spend my life saying I was too afraid to make good grades. I'm not going to pay myself off with a safety fix when I know what I need to do is take the risk of performing." I did take that risk, and I never looked back.

You'll also begin to think twice before impulsively behaving in a way that doesn't work for you. You'll begin to see more clearly down the road to the long-term consequences. You will find yourself weighing the pros and cons of things. When Friday night comes around, and your friends will want you to go drinking at a party, you'll be able to say to yourself, "What's the disadvantage of not drinking Friday night? I might miss out on some very temporary fun and I might lose some friends who will label me as boring. And what's the disadvantage of drinking? I might lose my car, my driver's license, perhaps my enrollment at a college if get arrested. I might also risk my life and the lives of others if I get in a car wreck." If you can do that before you go out to that party, there's a much greater chance you'll never take a single drink.

So what can you do to eliminate the payoffs that you listed earlier? Finish off with the following exercise.

1. ....

2. ....

3. ....

4. ....

5. ....

THE DANGER OF IGNORING YOUR PAYOFFS

I had a friend in high school who was always considered a really decent guy. But then one day he got caught trying drugs at a party, and his parents decided to send him off to a drug rehabilitation clinic just to be on the safe side. His parents had never been that active in his life. They both had high-powered, busy careers and had little time after work, but suddenly they were coming to the rehab center every day to see him. They agreed to meet with him for long family sessions. They took the time to express all their love for him.

Everybody figured everything was going to be okay. In fact, my friend came back to school and seemed to be a completely normal guy again. Everything returned to the way it used to be . . . until he was caught with drugs again and was sent back to drug rehab.

"What's the matter with you?" we asked him one day. "You're not the type to do drugs."

"I know, I know," he said.

I was too stupid at that point to ask my friend, if he knew he wasn't the type to do drugs, why was he doing them? What was his payoff? But I said nothing. I greeted my friend when he came back once again from drug rehab. He seemed like a nor-mal guy, without any real problems.

In fact, he seemed happier than ever because his parents had been there so often throughout his second stint at rehab. They encouraged him, they gave him a lot of love and attention, and they told him they'd be there for him regardless of how long it took.

One night at dinner my mom asked me, "I wonder if Will goes to drug rehab because of the attention he gets from his parents?"

"Huh?" I said.

"You know, his parents have never really been around. He's essen-tially been on his own all through high school. Maybe he's figured out a way to get their attention, to get them to stop their lives and be with him."

"By going to drug rehab?"

"Absolutely," my dad said; "that's his payoff."

I said nothing to Will about our conversation that night. Today, I wish I had. It might have snapped him back to reality. It might have made him realize that there might have been a better way to feel love from his parents than by risking his life with drugs.

He did more than risk his life. The drugs caught up with him and destroyed him. The summer after our junior year, I saw a newspaper headline referring to a teenager from my neighborhood who had been found dead of a drug overdose. I felt all the air go out of my lungs as I started reading the story. The dead teenager was my friend Will. The tragic truth was that Will died because of his blindness to his payoff system. What started as a cry for help became self-destructive, and in this case a fatal lifestyle. If he or his parents or his rehab therapist had realized that this was a cry for help on his part, perhaps he'd be alive today. But nobody bothered to analyze it and his life was the price he paid.

Now, Will's story is certainly more dramatic than yours, but I hope the story makes you realize that you must find your payoffs to your negative behavior. Take the time to understand what's going on in your own life. If you control your payoffs, you will start getting control of your life.

LIGHTBULBS

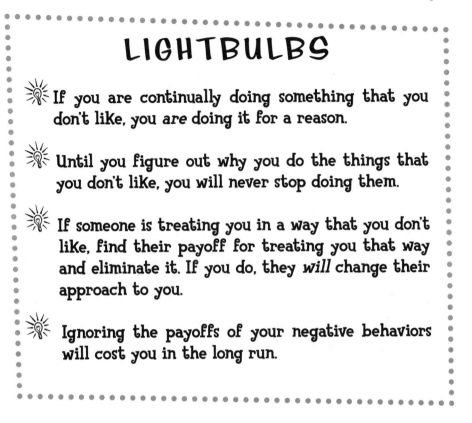

- If you are continually doing something that you don't like, you *are* doing it for a reason.

- Until you figure out why you do the things that you don't like, you will never stop doing them.

- If someone is treating you in a way that you don't like, find their payoff for treating you that way and eliminate it. If you do, they *will* change their approach to you.

- Ignoring the payoffs of your negative behaviors will cost you in the long run.

LIFE LAW FOUR

YOU CANNOT CHANGE WHAT YOU DO NOT ACKNOWLEDGE

You never find yourself until you face the truth.

—Pearl Bailey

To get real, quit living in denial so that you can open your eyes to what in your life is not working.

EMILY ABSOLUTELY HATES HISTORY CLASS. AND WHEN I say hate, I mean really, really hate. She would rather get a root canal than sit through boring discussions about dead people. But not wanting to totally waste time, she uses that period to read magazines or write notes to her friends. After all, that's kind of current history, right? If it's a magazine day, she takes her seat toward the back of the classroom, pulls out the magazine, and puts it inside her notebook. The teacher drones on and on, his voice a flat-line monotone. He's about as exciting as watching paint dry. "He's the worst," Emily tells her friends. "If I'm lucky, I fall asleep. Not that he ever notices. He just stands there head down reading his notes. He doesn't even know we're there."

Emily figures that her saving grace is that Mr. Excitement determines the victim's grades based entirely on two tests—the midterm and the final, so problem solved! On the night before the midterms, she starts to play catch-up. She grinds up some of her little brother's Ritalin, snorts it, and begins the well-known cramming drill. She studies all night, totally wired on the Ritalin. She is convinced that it is helping her remember all the facts, all the dates, all the historical figures she had not taken the time to read about during the semester—one night to cover one and a half months of material. No problem. Emily is feeling really confident that she is, no doubt, studying harder than anyone else in the class. "I have a deadlock on an A here," she tells herself, "how could I not. I have studied all night."

Just before class the next day, Emily slips into the girls' bathroom and snorts more Ritalin. "I worked so hard for this class," she tells her friends. "I studied all night. It's ridiculous how much work I have done for this one class. But I am ready." Indeed, she sails through the test, the first one in her class to finish. She is sure that she aced it.

Two days later, the tests come back: F—43. Emily has failed, and she has failed big-time. "How could that happen?" Emily complains to her friends, trying to hold back tears. "I pulled an all-nighter studying."

"Are you sure you were ready for that test?" a friend asks.

"No question," Emily says. "I worked so hard for that class, I was as ready as I could be. It's just not fair!" Now, maybe it's just me, but I think Emily might be full of it on this "ready as I could be" business. I think she may be conning herself and, in fact, is in complete denial about what it takes to get by in school.

DENIAL IS NOT JUST A RIVER IN EGYPT

Let me give you my definition of denial:

> **de-ni-al** \di-'ni-el\ *n:* Hardheaded, stubborn, and immature refusal to be honest with yourself about the stupid, insensitive, self-destructive things you do to jerk yourself around. Unwillingness to acknowledge problems because you wish they weren't there. Refusal to take ownership in whatever is not working in your life.

Pretty harsh, huh? But we all do it to some degree. We all trick ourselves about what's really going on in our lives. We also all trick ourselves about what's going *wrong* with our lives. But the moment we do that, we start hurting ourselves. We start killing our hopes and dreams. Because when we turn to denial, we kill what might have been a real chance to overcome a problem, and we kill the solution that might have worked if we had just tried. Life is full of obstacles, and if we pretend otherwise, they don't get removed or overcome. It's like ignoring a huge speed bump and hitting it at full speed; it ruins a smooth ride.

To deny your problems means to lie to yourself about those problems. You lie to yourself in two ways: (1) You make stuff up that isn't even almost true; and/or (2) you leave stuff out. Both forms of lying are equally dangerous. Not telling yourself that something is wrong and therefore letting it just build is sure to catch up with you. Emily was totally in denial about what she had to do to pass history. She did not want to have to study history every day so she remained in denial, telling herself that there was another way to get through the class. She conned herself into believing she could cram her way through the midterm. But you know—because you've been there—that a part of her knew the truth. A part of her knew that a bomb was going to hit on test day.

We're picking on her, but how about you? If you are living in denial about any part of your life, that simply means that you are not dealing with the parts of your life that are not working. Living in denial means that you are not giving yourself the chance to improve. So in keeping with my "harsh" definition of denial, here's some harsh advice: Stop BS'ing yourself! If you've got a problem, admit it! Get real! Pull your head out of the clouds and be honest! You are not a moron; you know exactly what's not working in your life, and you just need to find the guts to admit it so you can start changing it. And let me tell you, whatever is bothering you is not going to go away! I remember when I was a little kid, I used to think that if I closed my eyes you couldn't see me and whatever I didn't want to see would disappear. But of course we grow out of that, or do we?

If you're unwilling to acknowledge a problem or if you're unwilling to acknowledge a self-destructive emotion, it won't

go away even if you do have your "mental eyes" closed. How do you ever expect to change something if it doesn't get on your "to do" list? Lying to yourself is as dumb as going to a doctor who asks if you're having any pain anywhere, and you say no, even though one leg hurts like hell. What happens? The doctor doesn't deal with or treat your bum leg. How dumb is that? You killed any chance to get fixed, so you limp out the door the same way you limped in.

If you are living in denial, that is exactly what you are doing: You are killing any chance to fix the problem and you'll just keep on limping

through life. If you're a pain at school and no one wants to have you around, admit it. If you get unbelievably jealous and possessive of anyone you ever date, admit it. If you are so convinced that your parents are out to get you that there is no way you can ever get along with them, admit it. If you are incredibly lazy and spend every afternoon and evening listening to music or chatting online instead of studying, admit it. If you lie to people all of the time about what you did because you think your real life is a total bore, admit it. If you hate the way you are living your life, get real about it or it will never change. If you recognize that you are behaving in self-destructive or dangerous ways, have the guts to say so or you will never get it under control.

> Hold fast to dreams, for if dreams die, life is a broken-winged bird that cannot fly.
>
> —Langston Hughes

I saw some of my own friends deny themselves into trouble repeatedly. I had several friends in particular who did a lot of partying on weekends. Every Monday they'd come to school telling funny stories about how they went out drinking and what they did after they got drunk. At first, and by outward appearances, they seemed okay. Their weekend binge drinking didn't seem to have that big of an effect on them. Some of them were really drinking heavily and, inevitably, the

weekend binges began to affect their functioning the rest of the week as well. We all started to notice some major changes in my friend James. Even some of those who ran around with him on those wild weekends began to get nervous and change the way they were acting because of how they were seeing it affect James. He, of course, didn't see it as a problem at all. He was in denial. Life was one big party. I watched him lose his girlfriend because he acted like such a jerk when he drank. He would become rude and mean and she was totally repulsed by it. He didn't see it that way. He began to lose his edge on the basketball court because he was so out of shape. Teammates starting ragging on him because he wasn't holding up his end of the deal. Again, he didn't see the problem. His grades began going into the tank. Yet he just kept on partying. I finally mentioned it to him one time after practice and he just said, "Hey, I'm okay, don't sweat it. What are you, my mother?"

It soon got worse. James was drinking at a party that got totally out of control. We were at one of our friends' houses in a neighborhood that James didn't know very well, when, all of a sudden, the cops showed up and everyone took off running. James, who was by then staggering drunk, jumped a back fence, ran down a dark alley, made several turns, crossed a busy street, and found himself at a Taco Bell on the access road of a major highway. He had no idea where he was, and no money to call a taxi or a friend to come get him. He was lost and stranded. Finally, he started trying to find his way back to the house where the party had been taking place. There isn't a lot of foot traffic on major highways at night and a police car pulled up, stopped him, and started quizzing him on who he was and where he was going. James was barely coherent and had no good answers. He thought the party was on a street that started with an *L*, but was it Lindale or maybe Leland? He couldn't say. The nice officers decided to give James a little ride and a place to stay for the night.

He was arrested for public intoxication and taken downtown to the city jail, where he spent the night. The next morning the school and his parents were informed as to what had happened. This was not good for the life and times of James. He was suspended from school and kicked off the basketball team. This eventually resulted in the loss of an athletic scholarship to a great university. At one level, James knew he was spinning out of control, but he lived in denial because he didn't have the guts to get real with himself about what was happening. The price of denial for James was very, very high. He chose not to see until his world caved in, and by then it was too late.

Now, some of you out there may be saying, "Jay, I'm not running from cops. I'm not staggering around drunk at a Taco Bell alongside a highway in a major city. I am not that bad." Others of you may be saying, "Hell, that's a slow night." But whether or not you have major screwups in your life, you owe it to yourself to start asking some hard questions and take a serious look at how you might be putting yourself at risk or working to defeat yourself through what you are not seeing. Are you denying some really bad thinking and behavior? Are you putting obstacles in the road to block you from success? Maybe for you it's as simple as acknowledging that you hate it when your dad calls you "sweetie pie" in front of your teammates and your girlfriend so that you can ask him to stop.

It's time to get real about you and everything that is going on in your life, particularly everything that is not working in your life. Have the guts to be honest with yourself. Remember Life Law Two: You create your own experience. Well, through denial, you are creating a far more self-destructive experience than you even knew. Answer these questions:

1. **What am I doing to put myself, or allow myself to be, at risk in my life?**

....

....

....

2. **What am I doing that is Keeping me from succeeding?**

....

....

....

3. **How am I sabotaging myself in my relationships with parents and other adults?**

....

....

....

4. What am I doing to miss opportunities that I should be grabbing on to?

....

....

....

5. What do I need to change about my personality and behavior patterns?

....

....

....

Those are just some starter questions. I'll bet you know the others that you need to ask yourself.

DENIAL WORKS IN MYSTERIOUS WAYS

If your honest assessment tells you that your life isn't nearly off in the ditch like James's life was, that's great. But the whole idea is to do something *before* it gets in that situation and circumstance. Denial doesn't just sabotage people like James who refuse to see major problems. At one point, his problem wasn't that huge. But it became that way through denial and neglect.

To get to nowhere, follow the crowd.
—Charlie Brown

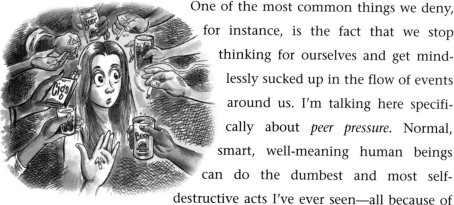

One of the most common things we deny, for instance, is the fact that we stop thinking for ourselves and get mindlessly sucked up in the flow of events around us. I'm talking here specifically about *peer pressure*. Normal, smart, well-meaning human beings can do the dumbest and most self-destructive acts I've ever seen—all because of peer pressure, the need to be accepted. I can't tell you how many times I have heard adults talking about their child getting into trouble because he or she "fell in with the wrong crowd." Now, I'm not making excuses for some dumb thing somebody did, and God forbid I get caught agreeing with a bunch of adults; but I have to tell you, I've seen time and time again where friends of mine who I knew to be pretty levelheaded stopped thinking for themselves and did really dumb things. They did it because they wanted to belong. They did it because they wanted to be cool and hang out with a certain group. They let the need to belong overcome common sense and good judgment. And so they screwed up big-time. They were vulnerable to the influence because they were in denial about their motivations. They denied their own warning and conned themselves into believing they really wanted to do the dumb thing. They didn't have the guts to admit that they wanted to belong so badly that they would go along to get along. They abandoned who they were and what they once valued. My dad always said, "If you don't stand for something, you will fall for anything."

Ask yourself what things in your life you have done because you felt pressure from your friends. Here's a list to start you thinking:

* **Being defiant and disrespectful to your parents because your friends are**

* **Being disinterested in school because only the "nerds" care about learning**

* **Drinking at parties because all the cool kids do**

* **Smoking marijuana or doing other drugs because it's the cool thing to do**

* **Having sex because it is expected and you don't want to lose the relationship**

* **Sneaking out at night because "everybody else" is doing it**

* **Lying to your parents about where you are going because "everyone else" is going to be there and you don't want to be left out**

Whether it was something on this list or some other behavior, did you wake up the next day, look in the mirror, and say, "How did I let that happen?" I'll tell you how it happened every time I did it: I denied my own voice, my own values, and substituted the judgment of some doofus for my own. I didn't remember Life Law One: You either get it, or you don't. People who get it *think for themselves*, because when the stuff hits the fan, Mr. Cool and his buddies never seem to be there to help shoulder the load.

This is a difficult issue, I know. On the one hand, you do want to try things; you want to take chances. But we all have to remember that there are consequences to our experimentation. There are moral and legal lines that we should never cross. Above all else, next time you are getting sucked in, remember, you might do these things with your friends, but when it comes time to pay the price, you pay it alone.

Don't be in denial about the power of peer pressure. It is perhaps the greatest influence in your entire life, and you are going to be faced with it daily.

If you at least acknowledge to yourself that you are being pressured, then you have a huge advantage. You can anticipate and prepare yourself to deal with it. You can decide ahead of time what to say to fight off the peer pressure. Take pride in the fact that you're not going to let anyone else run your life. Take pride in the fact that you know who you are, you know what you want, and that you are true to your values.

Take a minute and list five behaviors that you know you don't want to be a part of but you feel your peers are influencing you to do.

1. ....

2. ....

3. ....

4. ....

5. ....

Now list five comments you should be ready to say the next time you feel the pressure. Pretend you're talking to someone who's trying to suck you in.

1. I'm not going to do that because ....
2. I'm not going to do that because ....
3. I'm not going to do that because ....
4. I'm not going to do that because ....
5. I'm not going to do that because ....

Congratulations. You just took one more step out of denial.

THE COMFORT ZONE ISN'T SO COMFY AFTER ALL

What if you're someone who doesn't feel much peer pressure and, in fact, doesn't feel much pressure to do anything at all? It can be just as bad, however, to go too far in the other direction and become a total slug. You see, we also live in denial when we fail to admit to ourselves that we are not living up to our potential and are not creating something significant for our lives. What I mean by that is that you stop reaching for a higher level of achievement and accomplishment and pretend that your life is okay. You get up, brush your happy hair, throw on some clothes, drag yourself out of the house, and go through the motions of the day. You think you're comfortable, but you're not as happy as you could be. You're in what I call a "comfort zone" and you pretend that it's okay.

When you're in a comfort zone, you're living a life that is not really satisfying but is too comfortable to give up. It's a life where you might be doing "okay," but it's a life that also consists of little self-confidence or self-esteem, no sense of pride, and no action or initiative. You are living *risk free*.

The denial part kicks in because you lie to yourself about everything being great. You whine about parents, teachers, money, and every other excuse, totally denying your role in your life. You do it because by being in denial about the quality of your life, you keep yourself safe. If you admit that you want more, you are at great risk because now you have to go for more, and what if you fall flat? If you admit that you want to do better in school, have better friends, perform better in athletics, or have a better relationship with your parents, and then fail, you have admitted you are a loser. If you never admit that you want more, not having it won't be so painful. But once you admit it, there's nowhere to run and nowhere to hide. You are no longer living risk free. You don't get what you want living in the comfort zone, but at least it's not scary; that's why denial works.

Here are a few guidelines that you can use to determine whether or not you are stuck in a comfort zone:

* You're often bored with yourself.
* You feel that your accomplishments are pretty worthless.
* You think your daily after-school activities are mostly pointless.
* You don't seem to enjoy things the way other kids do.
* You make promises to yourself that you never keep.
* You have no goals.
* You're a little scared.
* You think your life doesn't have much of a purpose.
* You never challenge yourself.

Notice that these are not major problems that can destroy your life in one day, but they are problems that are like slow leaks in a boat. Your own boat won't go down like the *Titanic* but, slowly, it will sink to the bottom; and so will your life.

As long as you refuse to acknowledge even these small problems, they will gain momentum. As the months and years pass, these behaviors will become habits. Habits that will make your life less than what you want.

Remember that you are the only person who can change your life. If you want change, you're the one who's got to take action. If events in your life begin to flow differently, it will be because you have changed what you think, feel, and do. That will never happen unless you acknowledge that you need to make changes. Otherwise you will stay stuck. It's a simple truth: If you continue to do what you've always done, you will continue to have what you've always had. If you do different, you will have different.

GETTING OUT OF THE COMFORT ZONE

It is time to start thinking: What are the problems in your life that you have not been acknowledging? Don't go easy on yourself, saying what you want to be true about yourself as opposed to what is true. Don't give yourself the benefit of the doubt. You have to ask the hard questions and address the real issues that keep you from having everything you want in your life. Be sure that you are dealing with at least the following:

* **The parts of your personality that aren't working**
* **The parts of your behavior that aren't working**
* **The values and beliefs of yours that aren't working**
* **The relationships you have that aren't working**

The following exercises not only will help you confront your denial, but will help you make your first steps to get out of your comfort zone.

1. List the three things you are most unhappy with about yourself. What do you hate the most about who you are? For example: "My relationship with my parents."

    1. ....

    2. ....

    3. ....

2. How have you contributed to setting your life up that way? Take ownership in what's happened. For each quality you dislike about yourself, list what you have done to cause that unlikable quality. For example: "I'm not willing to listen to them. I blow up at anything."

    1. ....

    2. ....

    3. ....

3. Now describe what your life would be like if the undesirable aspect of your life was gone. For example, if the relationship was now perfect, you might describe it this way: "I can talk to my parents about my problems. They'd listen to me like an adult and respond like an adult."

1. ....

2. ....

3. ....

4. What is something you can do to move toward your perfect situation? For example: "I can refuse to blow up no matter what my parents say."

1. ....

2. ....

3. ....

I hope you are real with yourself. It's easy to say, "Hey, what am I supposed to do? I have no power, I have no control." But think back to Life Law Two: You create your own experience. You do have power, and you do have control. If you will acknowledge the areas you need to change, you can aim that power and control like a laser-guided missile and start making big changes. But it takes guts to get real with yourself about what needs to change about you and your life. Don't blame your parents. If you're playing it safe and not reaching, then you're lying to and cheating yourself and that's denial. If you aren't careful, you'll find the days turning into weeks, the weeks into months, months into years, and before you know it, you'll be so deep in a hole you won't know what to do.

Being honest means seeing the world, and your life, clearly. It's seeing the immediate threats that loom over your life, and it's seeing the potential problems just forming on the horizon.

One final thing: Don't get down on yourself because you are admitting you have problems. Your problems are just problems. You can be a no-good slug, but  because you have acknowledged what you're dealing with, you already have turned a corner. It doesn't mean that these problems define you. All you're saying is that you have work to do. So get excited. For the first time in your life you have a great chance to make changes—all because you are acknowledging what needs to be done. By showing the courage and commitment to be honest with yourself and to lay out for yourself exactly how things are, you are going to start breaking out of your comfort zone.

Remember the story about Emily at the beginning of this chapter? Well, fortunately, that F on the history test was a huge wake-up call for her. She got real after she received that 43 on her midterm. She acknowledged that she had a problem in history class and took action to fix her problem. She still hates history to this very day (and so do I), but I think one of the things we have to realize is that we don't have to like everything we do. Sometimes we just have to do it. She finally got mature enough to say, "History sucks and I absolutely hate it, but I'm gonna have to get to work or I'm gonna be taking it again and again and again."

Had she remained in denial about her ownership of the problem and continued to blame her poor grade on the boring teacher, she probably would have failed the class and wound up having to take it again. But she didn't. She realized that there was no way to make a good grade with one all-night, drug-assisted cramming session, so she decided to take control of her life. She said, "If I don't want to fail, I better start listening in class, reading the textbook instead of magazines, and staying awake while the teacher is talking, no matter how boring he is." It was tough for her to get out of her comfort zone, but it paid off. When the final came around at the end of the semester, Emily was ready. She made a high B and passed the course. Mission accomplished.

Emily took action, which is what you need to do. If you acknowledge and then take action to fix whatever problems you are facing in your life, then I promise you, you are on task in your life. You are dealing with things that matter. You are refusing to stay unhappy for another day. And that's what the next Life Law is all about, taking action.

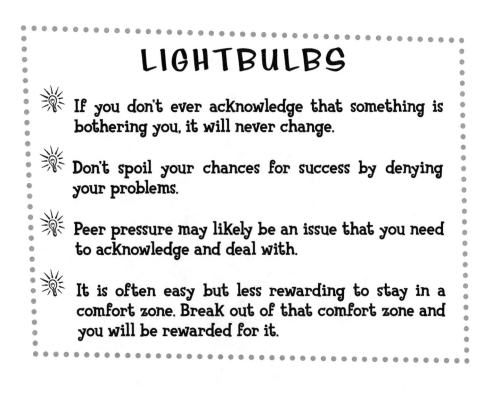

LIGHTBULBS

- If you don't ever acknowledge that something is bothering you, it will never change.

- Don't spoil your chances for success by denying your problems.

- Peer pressure may likely be an issue that you need to acknowledge and deal with.

- It is often easy but less rewarding to stay in a comfort zone. Break out of that comfort zone and you will be rewarded for it.

LIFE LAW FIVE

LIFE REWARDS ACTION

What you do speaks so loud that I cannot hear what you say.

—Ralph Waldo Emerson

WHY YOU SHOULD READ THIS LIFE LAW:

To become a person who makes decisions and acts on them. Stop floating along in the river of life.

WHEN I WAS IN HIGH SCHOOL, I WAS CRAZY about this girl Jennifer. Not only was she the best-looking girl on all seven continents, but she was the coolest girl ever. We were good friends and even dated some, and when it came time to ask a date to the senior prom, I really wanted to go with Jennifer. The problem was that the thought of asking her made me really nervous. Actually, it wasn't the asking part, but rather the answering part that I was so nervous about. I really did not want her to say no.

But as much as I didn't want to ask, I really wanted to go with her, so I got up the courage and asked. I almost wet my pants when I did, but I asked.

It turns out that Jennifer felt the same way about me as I did about her. In fact, not only did we go to the prom together, but I realized that she is the nicest, most caring person in the world, and we are still dating.

But I never would have known if I had not asked. By not asking, I not only would have ensured that I wasn't rejected (safety payoff!), but I also would have ensured that on prom night I would be sitting at home playing Jenga with my little brother and missing my opportunity to get to know the best possible girlfriend. Had I not taken action, I would have had no chance for success. But I did take action and my reward was a really good-looking date to the prom and, as it turns out, an awesome girlfriend. So I am living, walking proof that life does reward action.

So far in this book, we've talked a lot about having the life that we really want. But just remember that no matter how much you believe in the Life Laws, if you do nothing, you will have nothing.

There is an interesting formula in the adult version of *Life Strategies* that is real simple:

- ★ **Be**
- ★ **Do**
- ★ **Have**

What that means is that you must *be* committed, *do* what it takes, and then you will *have* what you want. In the earlier Life Laws, we talked about what it takes to be committed: acting accountable for your life, acknowledging all the things that you must change. Now it's time to *do*.

LIFE REWARDS ACTION

What I didn't understand was that if you offer up purposeless, meaningless, unconstructive actions, the world will respond to you with the same type of reactions.

What does that mean? It means no one cares about your bullshit.

I cannot emphasize this point strongly enough. You've got to get moving. One of the first things I had to recognize about myself before I could ever get the life I wanted was that my natural tendency was to make excuses. Whether I wanted to admit it or not, I would give myself permission to say what I wanted to do or intended to do, but then fall far short of actually doing it. It's human nature. It's the normal way of acting. We are a society of procrastinators. We wake up saying, "I'll do what needs to be done someday."

> Do or do not; there is no try.
> —Star Wars (Yoda)

But "someday" is not a day of the week. Intentions, or ideas without actions, are, I promise, your worst enemy. People don't care about what you mean to do. They only care about what you actually do. Your math teacher doesn't care if you "meant" to turn in your homework; your parents don't care if you "meant" to

clean up your room or come home by curfew; your dogs are not full if you only "meant" to feed them.

Don't forget, everybody around you "means" to do more. Everybody around you wants to be more than they are. Everybody wants to be the most popular girl or guy in school. Everybody wants to be a star athlete or a supermodel.

Yet sitting in your room living a fantasy life won't get you one bit closer to where you want to be. In fact, it can become a substitute for taking action. If you allow yourself to get really immersed in a fantasy life, you might find enough temporary gratification to undermine your motivation to do something for real. Instead of dealing with the reality that you are not doing squat, you escape into that fantasy world. You spend all day flipping through *Cosmopolitan* magazine wishing you could be like the girls in the photographs. You watch ESPN imagining how you would make that play. You get as many piercings as you can as part of your fantasy that you are making a "statement." Hey, sorry, making a temporary fashion statement is not the same as making real change. And that also goes for those of you who think wearing the right "in crowd" clothes will give you a better chance at being a success. You're fantasizing.

Are you fantasizing? Are you spending a lot of time daydreaming? Are you still coming up with excuses about why you haven't taken action? Or have you decided that you are not going to stay in the place where you are for one more minute?

RESULTS ARE THE ONLY MEASURING STICK

Measuring your success or failure purely as a function of results means that you measure your life based on what you do and what you get, not based on what you think and what you want. We live in a world that is constantly keeping score. And just like the scorekeeper at your high school basketball games, the world doesn't care if you meant to do something. The world only cares about what you have actually done. So start keeping score for yourself. Start making yourself take action to improve your life and get the things that you want. Nobody will do it for you. *You* have to do it, and you have to start now.

Angela, a longtime friend of mine, has always been one of the smartest and most talented girls I've known. She is not only loaded with brainpower, she is also really great to be around.

The problem is that she is now twenty-eight years old, and still living at home with her parents. She's gotten really heavy and doesn't date, and because most of her friends have moved out of their parents' neighborhood, she doesn't have anyone to hang out with and doesn't take the time to get out of the house to meet anyone.

You're thinking, "Oh, this is a story about a no-good slacker who doesn't have a clue." Wrong. Angela does not have to be told that she's got to get a grip and get her life moving. She's gone so far as to write down "plans" so that she can finally start living like an adult. She has a "plan" to get into medical school. She has a "plan" to start walking five times a week to lose weight. She has a "plan" to buy new clothes and to get a new image. And she has a "plan" to start going places to meet a boyfriend.

But she has never put into effect any of her excellent plans. Something has always tied her up. She hasn't been able to get to medical school because she doesn't have any money. She doesn't have any money because she can't get a job. She can't get a job because she needs to be studying for school. She can't lose weight because her mother is always making her cookies. And as long as she stays fat, it's pointless to look for a boyfriend, because she thinks no man would be interested in her.

Angela's problem is that she won't get started and she won't take action. Remember the be-do-have formula. Angela is being, but not doing. At this rate, she will never have. So do something. You can only create your own experience if you take action to do so. Planning is great, but doing is better. Take action immediately, because throughout our lives we are frequently presented with windows of opportunity. However, those opportunities will disappear whether we are ready for them to or not. We have to take advantage of the opportunities when we can.

I was always close to my grandfather, but in the eighth grade, when I started playing football, I just never got around to seeing him much. I meant to go see him, but I always got busy or got distracted and didn't go

do it. But for some reason, my dad forced me to take action and spend time with my grandfather. He recommended golf and practically forced me to play with my grandfather, to go to the movies with him, to go out to eat with him, and just to spend time with him. It wasn't odd that I was spending time with my grandfather, but it was odd that my dad was practically forcing me to do it. Looking back, I now see what my father was doing. He knew something I didn't. He had taken my grandfather to the doctor, and he knew that his days were numbered.

He knew that I would regret it if I continued to put off going to see him or going to spend some time with him. Luckily, I took my dad's advice and spent some time with my grandfather, because it was just a few weeks later that I lost him. Had I not spent time with him then, I wouldn't have had another opportunity to do so. Taking action paid off immediately right there. You will regret missing your own windows of opportunity. So do this little exercise for yourself:

1.   **List the five most important people in your life.**

1. ....

2. ....

3. ....

4. ....

5. ....

2.   **Now list what would be left unsaid if you unexpectedly lost those people.**

1. ....

2. ....

3. ....

4. ....

5. ....

3.   Now make a commitment to take action and go tell those people what you just wrote down. Set a time, set a place, set a method (whether it be by letter, telephone, or in person), but let them know exactly what you feel about them.

NO ONE WILL DO IT FOR YOU

For my first two or three years of high school, I consistently made Cs. I always wanted to make an A, but I guess I thought somebody would do the work for me. I had my C, and I felt like an A was on top of a one-hundred-story building and I couldn't even find the elevator. Now, granted, my first mistake was that I didn't realize that NBC wasn't educational TV. I guess I thought Conan O'Brien taught math, Dennis Miller taught English, and Jay Leno taught chemistry. But the major thing that I didn't realize was that eight weeks into the nine-week semester wasn't the best time to start studying. You just can't do that. I didn't realize that taking action on the first day of the semester would affect my grades at the end of the semester. I didn't realize that getting As on my homework would help me get As on my tests so that at the end of the semester I could get an A in the class. All I knew is I had a C, I wanted an A, and, hey, maybe I can sit up here in my room, and if I want it bad enough, I will just get it. But that simply won't happen. You have to take action and start climbing up that hundred-story building, floor by floor. Then before you know it you are at the top and you've got your A in your hand.

This is true with everything. Fantasizing that you made linebacker doesn't get you in any better shape. Wishing you lost ten pounds doesn't make you look better in your bathing suit. Wanting to be good at playing the trombone doesn't make you know the notes. With everything in life, you only get the things you work for. If you do nothing, you will get nothing. Life rewards action. Start moving now, because I can promise you that if you want to make the basketball team, the head coach is not going to get in his car, drive to your house, come inside, ask you to pause NBA 2000 on your Nintendo, and say, "Hey, why don't you come play basketball for us?" No matter how good you are or how good you look in a bathing suit, the world's not going to postpone try-outs, or summertime, just because you didn't take action soon enough. Although that would be great, it's not going to happen. You will never succeed if you don't at least try.

EMBRACING THE UNKNOWN

It's always easier and safer, though seldom rewarding, to spend our days not trying anything new. It's easier and safer because we are afraid that if we try something new we might fail or be rejected, and if that happened we would be miserable. However, not trying anything new often causes us to be just as miserable as failing at something new would. At least trying something new has the potential to make us happier.

This past semester I tried something new, and I am sure glad I did. As I was choosing my courses, I noticed that I had only chosen classes that were boring but that I thought would be easy. So I decided to take a risk—maybe not a big risk, but a risk—and try an astronomy class. Besides, how hard can it be? It's astronomy. I expected to look at some stars, maybe see some constellations. The hardest thing we should do in the class should be spelling "Uranus," right? Wrong!

Let me warn you, astronomy is a math course, and it's not fun math (as if there is such a thing). The first day of class, the teacher just casually said, "I want you to find the distance to the F-5 star of the Andromeda Galaxy. To do this, use the parallax, the inverse square law of light proportionality, and the Chandrasekhar limit. The question shouldn't be too hard."

I had no idea what this guy was talking about. I thought I had accidentally slipped into Greek class or something. So I started looking around and asking people if I was in the right place. Unfortunately, I was.

The risk I was taking kept getting bigger. I didn't have to take this class and could have switched to basket weaving or some other class that would be much easier. But I didn't. I decided to take a risk and stick with it. I knew that if I did well in this class, it would be much more gratifying than if I did well in basket weaving.

I stuck with that class for the entire semester and the teacher never did mention the Big Dipper. We spent the entire semester discussing some distant star galaxy that I have never heard of or care to again. I spent more time doing his homework, more time studying for his tests, and more time worrying about my grade in his class than any other. But while that may sound like the worst class of the semester, it wasn't. That was my best class of the semester. Because when I got my grade, regardless of what I got, I knew that I would be more proud of myself for completing that hard class than I would be for completing any other class.

Sure enough, my hard work paid off. I took action on the first day to start completing my homework assignments and learning the material, and though I would never take that class ever, ever again, I am very glad I did this time. I got a good grade, and although it was no better than any of my other grades, I was happier about that than any of the other grades I got the entire semester.

Decide that you're going to take some chances and then take action to ensure your success. Make a life decision to risk reasonably, risk responsibly, but risk. I'm not talking about skydiving here. I'm talking about letting yourself want more, and taking the action to get it.

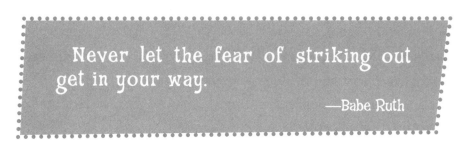

> Never let the fear of striking out get in your way.
>
> —Babe Ruth

Doing so, of course, means that you must have a conversation with yourself, something like the following:

* "There are obstacles." Yeah, there are obstacles, but I am going to get through them like a marine in boot camp.
* "Am I worth it? Can I do this?" You're damn right I am, just watch.
* "I may not succeed." Maybe not the first time.
* "I will be rejected." Not everything is handed to us the first time we ask. But persevering, until I get what I want, is the ultimate acceptance.
* "I will be a failure." I am a failure only if I don't try.

Resolve now that you will take the risk, make the effort, and be persistent in the pursuit of your goals. Your life should be filled with victories and rewards. If you are losing, that means somebody else is winning, so you know that winning happens. It might as well happen to you, but it's not going to happen by accident. It will happen because you make it happen. It will happen because you know what you want, and you move toward it in a strategic, consistent, meaningful, and purposeful manner. Take action and insist on results. This is a supremely important law of life.

To get you started, try the following exercise.

1. Imagine yourself finally volunteering at the homeless shelter, or even asking that guy you have always had a crush on out on a date. Write down three things you have always wanted to do, but never acted on.

1. ....

2. ....

3. ....

2.   Now write down three things that you can *do today* to make them happen.

1. ....

2. ....

3. ....

3.   Now go do them!

IT'S NO HILL FOR A CLIMBER

Don't be intimidated if what you want seems like an impossible challenge. Don't let yourself get overwhelmed by anything. It is easy to get intimidated. It may even seem as if your actions are failing, but be persistent. A friend of mine from high school is a perfect example of why you should never give up.

Ellen's parents divorced when she was fifteen. When her dad left, she was hit with the cold reality that she and her mother were going to have to support themselves. Her dad was abandoning them.

For Ellen, the disappointment was bitter. Her father soon left town, moved to another city, stopped nearly all personal contact with his children, and even stopped paying the minimal child support he owed the family. Ellen's family struggled to pay the bills and Ellen had to do without many things that other teenagers take for granted—like new clothes every now and then. Ellen had hoped for a scholarship to get to college, but because she was having to work so many after-school jobs, she wasn't able to keep on top of her studies and had only average grades.

Ellen wasn't ready to quit, however. She came up with one more plan. After high school, she would take a year off, working full-time to save enough money for a year of college. Then throughout college, she worked a couple of part-time jobs on her way to her college diploma. This was a girl who was often tired, who was often discouraged when she saw how much easier it was for her fellow students who had parents to pay for things, but she kept her mind focused on her goal and did not give up. Ellen understood that if she just kept trying she would eventually succeed.

Ellen never gave up, and neither should you. Take action today and you *will* be successful tomorrow.

LIGHTBULBS

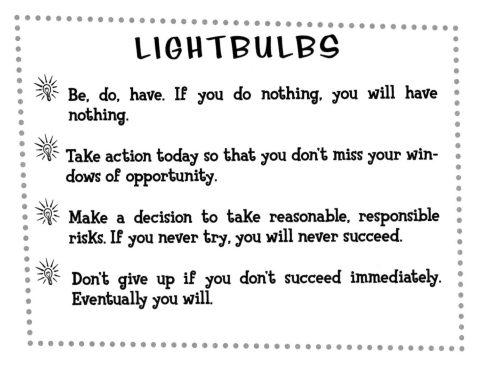

- Be, do, have. If you do nothing, you will have nothing.

- Take action today so that you don't miss your windows of opportunity.

- Make a decision to take reasonable, responsible risks. If you never try, you will never succeed.

- Don't give up if you don't succeed immediately. Eventually you will.

LIFE LAW SIX

THERE IS NO REALITY, ONLY PERCEPTION

You can complain because roses have
thorns, or you can rejoice because thorns
have roses.

—Ziggy

WHY YOU SHOULD READ THIS LIFE LAW:

*To find out if you have a warped view of your life. Get in focus so you
can hit the bull's-eye.*

WOULDN'T IT BE WEIRD IF YOU LIVED YOUR
whole life seeing the world as you think it is now, with
green trees, blue sky, and people with two eyes, two
ears, a nose, and a mouth, and then someone came along and suddenly
popped some lenses out of your eyes and the whole world looked different? The sky would turn purple, trees would be blue, and people would

look like creatures from outer space. You'd probably feel a little like you were in the movie *The Matrix,* in which the main character finally realizes that what he thinks is reality is, in fact, a computer-induced image.

Well, in this Life Law, you're about to learn that such an idea isn't a fantasy you see only in the movies. When I say there is no reality but only perception, I'm not exaggerating just to be dramatic. The fact is that everyone sees the world differently—*very* differently. I'm not trying to get cosmic on you. What I mean is that our emotions—like fear, or anxiety, or unhappiness, or depression—are based only upon our "perceptions" of what is happening to us. The interpretations that we make of the events of our lives, and the reactions that we have to them, are all that matters. In other words, no matter what happens in your life, how you interpret those events is up to you.

If you don't think this Life Law is true, then think about something you do on a typical day. Let's say you walk into the school cafeteria and someone you've always liked but never gotten a chance to know casually says "hi" to you. You immediately start trying to interpret to yourself what that "hi" means. Was that person flirting with me? Was that "hi" an invitation for me to say "hi" back and sit with that person at one of the cafeteria tables? Was that "hi" said just because I happened to walk right in front of that person and he or she wasn't sure what to say? Or was that person actually saying "hi" to someone right behind me?

It's exhausting, isn't it? But you play that game with yourself all the time, don't you? You don't react to what happens to you (in this instance, someone saying "hi"), but you react to your interpretation of what happens to you (in this instance, how you interpret what that "hi" means). How you see and interpret certain events is purely a matter of choice. All that there is . . . is perception.

Henry Ford once said, "If you think you can, or if you think you can't, you are probably right." If your perception of yourself is that you can beat back any fear, then you are right. If your perception of yourself is that fear is going to overtake you, you are right. My older cousin, Scott, worked one summer as an orderly at a mental hospital, and he told me a story about a guy on the ward whom everyone called Woody. Woody was one of the few patients who had visual hallucinations. He would "see" monsters. His therapist asked

him one time to draw what he saw, and Woody, a pretty gifted artist, drew these unbelievably frightening creatures, with huge heads, fangs, dripping saliva, and claws for hands. One day in his room, he started screaming that the monsters were coming after him. Two orderlies headed to his room, thinking they could just calm him down and reason with him until he realized that there really were no monsters. But he never stopped kicking and yelling. Suddenly, he collapsed with a heart attack. His perception of a life-threatening monster was so real that his experience was the same as if he had actually been fed to the monster. I was stunned. My cousin said Woody would probably have died from his perception of reality had it not happened in a hospital.

The story is dramatic, but it's also symbolic of all of us. It's not necessarily the actual events of our lives that shape us, but our perceptions of those events. Many times our perceptions are very distorted rather than clear, self-defeating rather than constructive.

That's why a big question you must always keep asking yourself is whether or not the lenses through which you view the world are clear, giving you a clean and factually based view of your life, or are they tinted or out of focus in some way? What if all the things you perceive to be true are not really, well, true? What if all the people in the world, like teachers, parents, friends, or relatives, aren't actually as weird as you think they are? What if they really don't think you're as weird as you think they do? What if they like you more than you think they do? What if you like them more than they think you do?

THE LENSES WE USE

Let's start by trying to figure out what lens you're using. Everybody has a general lens through which to see the world. Read the following descriptions and see which one, or which combination of descriptions, you think best describes your general point of view toward life.

The Me Lens

This is a lens in which everything that happens in the world is evaluated in terms of how it affects you. You evaluate things in terms of what's in it for you or what impact something will have on you.

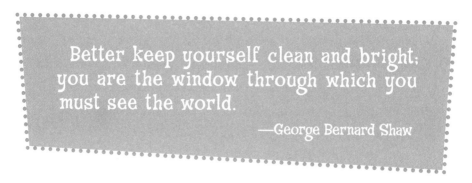

Better keep yourself clean and bright; you are the window through which you must see the world.

—George Bernard Shaw

The Peer Lens

This lens causes you to evaluate your entire world based on what others think about you. If you feel you have gained peer approval, you feel successful. You're the type who thinks there is nothing more important in life than being accepted by the right group of friends. They are the foundation to your life.

The "I'm in Love" Lens

This is somewhat similar to the Peer Lens, but it's worse. In this lens, everything in your life is dependent on having a boyfriend or a girlfriend. You totally measure your self-worth as a function of whether somebody else is in love with you or not.

The Material Lens

This lens causes you to relate to the world in a comparative way. You are totally tuned in to material wealth and focus on what your possessions are versus the possessions of others.

The Achievement Lens

You measure your self-worth totally as a function of what you have accomplished. You are obsessed with grades, club and committee membership, and awards or distinctions in your life. There is little room for evaluating yourself or others on the basis of character.

The Authority Lens

This lens causes you to be totally focused on how you are relating to those in your life who have authority. You are either obsessed about gaining their approval, or you are equally obsessed with rebelling against their control. Either way, your obsession dominates your every thought, feeling, and action.

The Victim Lens

Viewing the world through this lens causes you to be obsessed with how you are being hurt or victimized by the world. Things are seldom, if ever, your fault, and you tend to believe that the world is, in fact, out to get you.

The Hate Lens

With this lens, you see enemies behind every tree, waiting to drag you down. You know that when people say something nice to you, there is probably a hidden motive somewhere.

The Safety Lens

You see life as a place where it's better to be safe than sorry. You never take a risk because you don't trust yourself to handle the pain of failure.

The thing about all of these lenses is that they give you a very decided view of the world. But most important, they are all based on choices you have made about how you see the world. Remember, you can change your lenses.

1. What are the lenses that you use in your life? ....

2. How does it make your life better? ....

3. How does it make your life worse? ....

I HEAR VOICES

It's not just the way you see that's critical in determining your perceptions of the world. It's the way you talk—to yourself, that is. Try to imagine a giant tape recorder being inside your head, always on, always playing audiotapes, twenty-four hours a day. On the tapes are the thoughts, feelings, and beliefs that you have experienced so many times that they may occur without your even taking conscious notice of them.

These tapes are huge influences on us. We are with ourselves all day and all night, and if we are always letting the tapes playing in our head put us down or put other people down, then think of the devastating effect they can have.

In my focus groups, I asked both guys and girls to search through their minds about different topics. Here was a question I asked the girls: "Girls, what are the things that you just automatically, reactively feel and believe about boys in general?"

Here were the answers:

- ★ "Guys are jerks."
- ★ "All guys care about is one thing—sex."
- ★ "Guys don't want to talk about feelings."
- ★ "If you can't bounce it, hit it, or throw it, guys aren't interested in it."
- ★ "Guys are whiners."
- ★ "Guys are a lot of fun if you can trust them."
- ★ "Guys are macho and insecure."

The guys were then asked what they automatically, reactively felt and believed about girls in general. Here were their answers:

- ★ "Girls are two-faced."
- ★ "Girls gossip constantly."
- ★ "You can't live with them and you can't live without them."
- ★ "Girls are like bottomless pits; they are never satisfied."
- ★ "Girls are too emotional."
- ★ "Girls are high maintenance."
- ★ "Girls will take you away from your friends and your interests."

I also asked for a reaction to another topic: teachers.

- ★ "Teachers have too much authority."
- ★ "Teachers do as little as possible to get by."
- ★ "Teachers don't care about you as an individual."
- ★ "Teachers are losers or they wouldn't be teaching."
- ★ "Teachers are arrogant."
- ★ "Teachers? Do you mean torturers?"

Finally, I asked the same question about parents:

- ★ "Parents don't listen."
- ★ "Parents don't take you seriously."
- ★ "Parents are lovable but not likable."
- ★ "Parents are self-absorbed."

- ★ "Parents always say no."
- ★ "Parents would rather ignore you than deal with you."
- ★ "Parents love controlling you."
- ★ "Parents give up too easily."

What you just read were essentially our "tapes"—the thoughts we automatically have about guys, girls, teachers, and parents. The tapes are based on what we have experienced (or think we have experienced) in the past. But the question is: How accurate are these tapes for the here and now?

Think about this. You might know a guy who's a jerk, or a girl who's self-absorbed, or a teacher who's cruel, or a parent who won't listen, but a problem takes place if you start to use those past negative experiences with others as the basis for the "tapes" playing in your head. The problem is that these tapes, based on the past, are telling you what to think about the here and now. Go back through all of the statements that the girls expressed about guys. If those statements are unconsciously playing over and over in their heads—if they have become "tapes"—then whenever those girls approach a potential romantic relationship, they are going to have less chance for success. Their tapes have obviously set that relationship up for failure before it ever has a chance to survive. They've already got their conclusions in place about what guys are like before they meet a new guy.

The same thing goes for your relationship with your parents. If you approach your parents with your negative parent "tapes" playing, there isn't going to be much room for that relationship to grow. You've already got your conclusions in place about who your parents are. You don't listen. You come to every interaction with a closed mind.

Even if you think your thoughts are positive, your negative tapes can overwhelm you and prevent you from evaluating your current situation as it actually is. Because these tapes are playing so regularly, you have trouble believing that there could be another kind of reality. You don't seek additional information about what could be happening. All you do is look for that information that confirms what you already believe to be true.

You do this all the time. If you're a guy, you meet a girl, you like her, but she cries during a sad scene when you take her to a movie on a date. Because your tapes are playing, you think, "She's too emotional, like all other girls. I'm not going to like her." If you're a girl, and the tape in your head is saying that all guys just want a girl to put out, you're going to have your radar set up to perceive any action by a guy as consistent with what you believe to be true. Let's say you're on that movie date and the guy reaches for some popcorn that you are holding in your lap. You're going to think, "He is reaching for my boobs!" If you never give guys a chance, you'll never discover that a whole lot of them out there are actually interested in the popcorn and aren't just trying to cop a feel.

YOUR TAPES ABOUT YOURSELF

You need to be careful not only of the tapes you play about your friends, family, and teachers. You have to be especially careful about the tapes that you play about *yourself*.

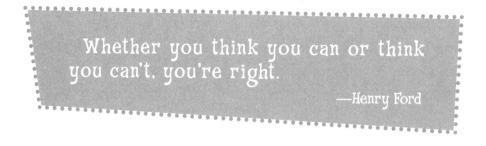

Whether you think you can or think you can't, you're right.

—Henry Ford

If you're thinking negatively about yourself—if you are lacking self-esteem, self-confidence, and self-inspiration—then you know you've got some negative tapes playing. What if you are getting ready to run a race, or try out for a play, or ask for a date, and all of your automatic thoughts are saying things like, "I'm not good enough," and "I'm not as deserving as everyone else," and "I know I can't do this"? Then what do you expect to happen when you throw yourself into the arena?

The problem is not the reality of your life. It's what you're telling yourself about your life. Assume your inner tapes are telling you things, over and over, like the following:

1. I'm not smart enough.
2. These other people are much more interesting than I am.
3. No matter what I do, it won't make a difference.
4. I'm just going through the motions; nothing will ever change.
5. People will soon figure out how dumb I am.

Now, I don't want you to start acting like the football coach at your high school who shouts into the microphone at pep rallies, "Let's be winners, boys and girls!" But I do want you to recognize that allowing certain taped messages to keep running in your brain will doom you to a life of mediocrity. The obstacles that you can build in your mind with this kind of talk are impossible to overcome. Listening to those tapes often makes you your own worst enemy. If, on the other hand, you evaluate everything in the here and now, you are always open to the possibility of success.

A NEW, BETTER PERSPECTIVE

You can tell yourself right now that you no longer have to live with the "interpretation" you have put on your life due to your past. All you have to do is make the decision to change your perceptions. When you do that, your skewed lenses and your negative tapes will soon get tossed aside, and you'll start seeing life from a clearer, more factual perspective.

One way to break your lenses and your tapes is by challenging your assumptions. Let's say you view life through the Hate Lens or that you have serious negative tapes playing about the opposite sex. You're a girl who genuinely thinks all guys are jerks. Challenge the assumption. Say to yourself, "My belief that all boys are jerks is only my perception. The next guy I meet is an individual and I'm going to evaluate him on his current conduct, values, and beliefs. If he turns out to be a jerk, fine, I'll call him that. But it will be because of what he does in the here and now. I won't bury him based on a generalization."

Let's say you view life through the Me Lens. You are the most important thing in your life, to the exclusion of anyone else. Challenge that assumption. If everything that happens in your life seems to revolve around you, what a terrible burden that can be. If your parents get a divorce, it is about you. If your family has money problems, it is about you. No matter what happens, you burden yourself with everything being about you. Choose to take a more realistic approach and find out what the real problems are.

A new perspective on life means you've got to make decisions based on the here and now and recognize that you no longer have to base decisions on what happened to you last year. What's important to do is to start talking to yourself the right way. It's very easy to knock down the obstacles in life with the right kind of inner dialogue. Your attitude in life is your choice—and your choice only. I don't care what kind of rules or restrictions are upon you right now. I don't care how mean your teachers are. I don't care if your parents don't understand you. I don't care if the world dealt you a lousy hand compared to some rich kid down the street. You choose how to respond to your situation.

IT'S YOUR VOICE

Never forget one thing. *You* are the voice of your life—not your past, and not someone else. It is through your voice, and your voice alone, that you will find the determination to make yourself a success. You can't rely on other people's inspirational voices. You can't rely on a great motivational speech now and then. You have to rely on your voice. You are the only person who can change your perception of yourself and your life.

LIGHTBULBS

- Your emotions are based on your perceptions of what is happening to you. If you perceive something as scary, then to you, it *is* scary.

- Your perception of the world is based on the lenses through which you see things. You can, however, change your lenses.

- Don't be influenced by your personal tapes. Evaluate everything based on what is currently happening.

- You are the only person who can change your perception of yourself and your life.

LIFE LAW SEVEN

LIFE IS MANAGED; IT IS NOT CURED

We are what we repeatedly do. Excellence, then, is not an act, but a habit.

—**Aristotle**

To figure out how to get it going and keep it going. Learn to program yourself rather than hope for success.

YOU NOW HAVE SIX LIFE LAWS UNDER YOUR belt and that's great. But as important and powerful as these first six Life Laws are, there is one thing that they will not do for you. They will not keep you from having problems. You have always had problems and you always will. There is never going to be a time in your life when you will just wake up and have a problem-free life. There's always going to be some dork at school messing with you, some teacher who thinks it is his personal mission in life to make you miserable, or your parents or brothers or sisters seemingly sabotaging everything you try to do. It's going to happen. Problems are just part of life.

I'm not trying to discourage you here. I am just being honest. It would be naive to think that because you've learned how the world works means your life is going to be smooth sailing from now on. The key is to not panic or think you have done something wrong when you do encounter problems. I don't want that to happen. When problems come up I want you to say to yourself, "I can handle this." That's exactly what this chapter is about: What are you going to do to actively manage your life and all the problems that come with it?

Let's start out this chapter with a clear understanding. If your problems are important to *you*, then they *are* important. I hate it when people try to belittle my problems by saying stuff like, "Don't think of your problems as problems; think of them as challenges." Or what about the old line, "Your problems are nothing more than opportunities to distinguish yourself"? Oh, and here's one that really makes me mad: "You think you have problems? You don't even know what problems are. Let me tell you about problems . . ."

The problems you and I have are real problems, whether it's too much acne on our face or some guy in math class who wants to whip our ass after school. I'm not going to play mind games with you by suggesting that our problems are not real because we're still young and not yet adults. Perhaps you have heard that old adage that says: "I was sad that I had no shoes until I met a man who had no feet." Well, yes, that statement does put our problems in perspective.

We definitely don't need to overdramatize our problems, but belittling them doesn't make them go away; they are still our problems and that counts. Don't feel guilty because you are concerned over having no date to the prom when there are millions of children suffering in third-world countries. If you are sensitive to those children, as you should be, work to help them. But you still need to get a date to the prom. In other words, you and your problems count and they are worthy of your efforts and energies.

FINDING A WAY TO DEAL WITH IT

It doesn't matter what your problem is. There is a way for you to deal with it if you will just work at it. Successful people aren't successful because they don't have problems. They are successful because they know how to deal with their problems. They make a plan to deal with each new problem rather than denying or ignoring that it exists. Or to put it another way, they "manage" their lives.

You have to be your own life manager, and you are the only life manager you will ever have. That means you can't fire yourself if you are doing a bad job. You can only improve on the job you are doing. That is what this Life Law is all about: you becoming a better life manager. What you're about to learn is how to confront your problems head-on and deal with them constructively rather than creating a whole new set of problems due to your reaction or lack of reaction to the original problem.

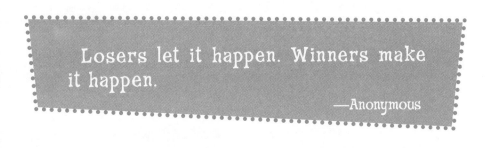

Losers let it happen. Winners make it happen.

—Anonymous

I'm betting that you are probably not a great life manager right now. That's okay because it is a learned skill. You aren't born a good life manager. You have to learn how to do it. Unfortunately, there are all kinds of ways to do it poorly, and you usually end up doing that first. Look around and notice what kinds of poor management strategies you see people using. Here are some you might recognize:

★ *Paws-up Strategy:* These people are like the dog that has been whipped so much that every time you walk up to it, it just rolls over on its back  and whimpers. These people do the same thing. Every time a problem arises, they just quit; they do the emotional equivalent of rolling over on their back and just wait to see how bad it is going to get. If it passes, fine. If it doesn't, they just lay there and take it. It's like they love being the victim; they just won't help themselves. They wouldn't yell "Fire!" if they were on fire!

★ *Ostrich Strategy:* Pure, 100 percent denial. These are the people  who won't even look at their test scores. If the teacher is returning tests and puts them on the desk facedown, they just stuff them in their backpacks and never even take a look at how they did.

★ *MTV Strategy:* These people acknowledge problems, but are going to deal with them only after they watch a little MTV. The problem is, they never seem to quit watching.

* *Cutesy Strategy:* Very popular among girls who put on innocent, little-girl faces and voices when they have a problem: "Oh, Mommy, I thought you said I could take all your money out of your purse without asking."

* *Inner-child Strategy:* When you get in trouble, just blame it on your upbringing or your parents' having trouble at home or your little sister (or brother) going through a great crisis of her own that is requiring your attention. You are just *soooo* bottled up inside, you just can't seem to help yourself.

* *Who-me? Strategy:* Nothing is your fault; everything happens because somebody else was out to get you or he was stupid or it was just really bad luck. But it certainly wasn't you.

So what's been your strategy so far? Is it one of these or were you even more creative than that?

I guess I don't have to tell you that if you are managing your life in any of the above ways, that is not a good thing. The world runs on results and your life and the job you are doing should be rated no differently. Baseball managers, for example, are quickly gauged on their win-loss records—not on their personalities, their great sound bites, or how good they look spitting tobacco in the dugout; results are the only yardstick the world uses for measuring how well they are doing. And like it or not, the world uses that same yardstick with you.

Think about yourself as a life manager, as though you were a separate person who had been hired to manage your life. Pretend that you are calling that separate person in for a life management performance evaluation. Remember that the only real measure is results as you evaluate this "separate" person who is your life manager. Here are some key questions:

1. Is your life manager making informed decisions?
2. Is your life manager letting you show people what you can do best?
3. Is your life manager putting you in the right place at the right time, or the wrong place at the wrong time?
4. Is your life manager taking care of you physically, mentally, emotionally, and spiritually?
5. Is your life manager selecting good relationships for you?
6. Is your life manager urging you to not live in a comfort zone?
7. Is your life manager designing your day so that you have some free time to relax?
8. Is your life manager allowing you to get dates and meet new friends?
9. Is your life manager putting your life together in a way that you are having fun and enjoying yourself?
10. Is your life manager creating your experiences in a way that you feel good about who you are and what you are doing?

Those are the kinds of things that a life manager is supposed to be doing for you. So, as your only and therefore most important client, how are you doing?

DOING IT THE RIGHT WAY

Let me emphasize: Managing your life is not an event; it is a process. You will never "fix" your life. As the law says, life is managed; it is not cured. You must always keep working at making your life better and figuring out a better way to manage your problems.

Even when your life seems to be about as good as it could possibly get, you have to manage it with purpose and drive. You cannot stop moving. You might think you're leading the parade at the moment, but if you don't keep moving your feet, your butt is going to be back in the tuba section before you know it. I cannot say this strongly enough. Once you begin to "get it"—once you begin to understand how you can put your life together so that you are in charge of what happens to you—there is a natural tendency to relax. You know you've made some progress, you know you've gotten down some strong fundamentals from previous chapters, you know you've developed some new insights into the way you behave. But don't stop working now. Life management, as I said, is a process.

I've never seen a winner or a champion who was coasting in life. A few years ago, I saw a great example of someone who really understood this Life Law. This guy sure looked as if he had it made, but he was working more actively as a life manager than other guys who obviously did not have it made. He seemed to be as good as he could possibly be, but he didn't stop trying to improve. He obviously saw that the management of his life was a process that went on and on, no matter how well he was doing. I watched him in a highly competitive environment and he was clearly head and shoulders above everyone else around. But even though he was clearly superior, he was working harder than everyone else. The others would do their job and go home. But not him. He would do his job and would meet and master the challenge, but then he would stay hours after everyone else had gone home, working harder and harder so he could do even better the next day. Nobody knew that he was putting out the extra effort except him, but he did it anyway.

That person was Tiger Woods. Here was arguably the best golfer ever to play the game, winning the tournament by a wide margin, and when everyone else had gone home, he was still working, managing short-comings and building on strengths. He was all alone on the practice tee at the end of the day, hitting, hitting, and hitting some more.

There is more to Tiger's story. Tiger was not born a champion and he did not wake up one day all pumped up, deciding that he was going to go out and make himself into a world champ through sheer willpower and desire. What he created for himself was a "program."

I promise you, attaining your long-term goals takes more than willpower and desire. I know this thinking runs counter to what you have heard all of your life. You want to lose ten pounds. "You need willpower" is what everyone tells you. You want to pass a test; you need willpower. Willpower doesn't work because it comes and goes.

Getting all pumped up and having the willpower to do something might work for a few days, but then when the emotions are gone and

you don't "feel" like it anymore, you go right back to where you started. Willpower almost always fizzles out. You need, instead, a *program* that will become a part of your life, a program that will carry you whether the emotions are there or not. If you are going to be successful at losing weight and keeping it off, or getting good grades, instead of *a* good grade, you have to program your life and your world in a way that sets you up for success. That means changing your environment, time schedules, commitments, routines, activities, and objectives. Whatever your life now includes, your world has been set up in such a way as to support that. If you want different, you are going to have to program different. The key is getting the job done whether you feel like it or not. Nothing short of setting up your world in a way that is geared to success will get you to where you want to go.

Willpower is good only for short-term, onetime deals. Willpower is what gets you to lose weight in two weeks so you'll look good for a dance. But willpower is never going to be enough to keep the weight off. I don't care how pumped up and excited you might feel about something; that energy is going to fade. You'll gain the weight back after two weeks. You'll get yourself back into a hole in school again where you are late on your next paper.

What you need to do is stop relying on a short-term burst of energy and start creating a permanent lifestyle where you can't help but change and improve the flow of your life.

So how do you do that?

PUTTING YOUR LIFE ON PROJECT STATUS

To be consistently successful, you have to put your life management on high priority. I call it putting yourself on "project status."

When something is on project status, that means that it is top priority. It means that you make a specific plan and you commit to it. It means you devote time and energy. If you're like me, you've got lots of ideas for things you want to do and things you'd like to be. Whether it's having a better relationship with your parents or being a great student, you might typically find yourself thinking about how great those things would be. But just as Life Law Five says, it won't ever happen until you make it happen and, more important, keep it happening.

That's what living in project status is all about. The matter at hand takes on special significance. Think about improving your grades. Every day you say, "I've got to get better grades." But if you said, "Project status: I have to study before I talk on the phone to Arthur," then the difference in your rate of progress would be amazing. Otherwise, Arthur would become a long-lost friend.

And by the way, don't feel selfish about putting yourself at the top of the priority list. If you don't take care of yourself and manage your life, then it won't get done. It's not selfish to put yourself at the top of your priority list because you can't give away what you don't have. The better you take care of yourself, the better you manage your life, the more you can and will give to others in your life. At first, those parts of your life that you focus on will be the things necessary to get you on your feet mentally, emotionally, socially, physically, and spiritually. But soon, as you do a better job of managing your personal life, you will move on to managing the interactive parts of your life, and those around you will benefit greatly.

SO WHAT ARE PRIORITIES MADE OF?

A big part of coming up with a strategy for managing your life is knowing who you are and how you feel about some important dimensions of living. We always hear people talk about values and beliefs. To me that used to be the signal for "nap time." But the truth is, you and I have values and beliefs as well; we just don't talk or think about them much. They are decisions that we have made about what we will and won't do in our lives and what standards we will hold ourselves to. Sometimes it is as simple as personal pride.

All of that is a long-winded way of saying that we have already made a number of what are called life decisions. Life decisions are different than daily decisions in that they take place at the heart level rather than the head level. We use our heads to decide what we want for lunch; we use our hearts to decide what really defines us in this world. These heart decisions tend to stick because they aren't easy to make. I'll bet that you have made life decisions that you probably didn't realize and don't even think about anymore. For example, haven't you made the decision that you won't be mean and cruel to animals? Have you made a decision that you won't steal money from your friends? You are probably thinking, "Of course!" And you are right. Those are simple things that you don't debate every single day. They are life decisions that define you and your integrity. What I am asking you to do now in becoming an active manager is to make some more life decisions.

In fact, what are the life decisions that you can and need to make now that will improve the quality of your life and the efficiency with which you manage it? These life decisions may very well be things that cause you to require more of yourself than you now do. That's okay. That's what being a good life manager is about: getting more of what you want and less of what you don't want. These new life decisions will become the basis of your new management strategy. They will be unique to you and highly important. Here are some examples of life decisions that I have made or my friends have made that might help you get started:

* I will not drink and drive.
* I will not take advantage of or make fun of people less fortunate than myself.
* I will not steal what is not mine.
* I will not blame others for my problems or shortcomings.
* I will treat people with dignity and respect.
* I will live with passion.
* I will utilize my mind and my body.

Let's do a little work. First, write down five life decisions that you are already conscious of and that you know are part of your life.

1. ....

2. ....

3. ....

4. ....

5. ....

Now list five life decisions that you would like to make part of your life. Understand, these are not casual commitments you are making. These are major principles by which you will always manage your life.

1. ....

2. ....

3. ....

4. ....

5. ....

TURNING DREAMS INTO GOALS

There is one last trick to make sure that you begin to manage your life proactively rather than just waking up every day and simply reacting to what happens. If you want different, you have to do different. And you have to do different in a purposeful, strategic way.

Everybody dreams of what might be. Everybody fantasizes about wonderful events and circumstances in his life. It's like going to a movie but the movie plays in your mind instead of on a screen. It's great entertainment and it can be a lot of fun. But how about turning these dreams into reality? How about making this movie in your mind come true?

> The dictionary is the only place success comes before work.
>
> —Anonymous

How about turning those dreams into goals? The big difference between a dream and a goal is that dreams are kind of fuzzy and vague and goals are very clear and specific. Here are seven steps that you must take to turn your dreams into goals.

★ *Translate your dream into specific events or behaviors that define what you want.* It is not enough to say you want to be a good student. You have to define "good student" specifically and behaviorally. What does it mean in the real world?

★ *Translate your dream into things that you can measure.* For example, if you want to have a better body, what does that mean? How many pounds must you lose, what size do you want to be, what measurements do you want to have? Translate your dream into measurable outcomes.

★ *Assign a timeline to your goal.* "Someday" is not a day of the week. You have to make a commitment to when you want what you want. By setting a timeline to your goal, you will hold yourself to a schedule rather than just hoping that it will happen "someday."

★ *Choose a goal that you can control.* Unlike dreams in which you fantasize about all manner of things, some of which you can't possibly control, a goal has to involve things to which you have access. There is no point in setting a goal to be taller so you can be a better basketball player. (If I could have figured out how to get taller, I would have done it a long time ago.) But what you

can do is to set a goal to "play big." You can build your legs up so strong that you can jump higher than somebody a foot taller than you. That's something you can control.

★ *Plan a program and a strategy that will get you to your goal.* If you don't have a plan to get you from where you are to where you want to be, you will never get there. Think of the difference in the way you move when you are just strolling around killing time versus how you walk when you are hurrying to get somewhere. The progress you make is dramatically different. Have a plan to get your goals, and you will move like you have somewhere to go.

★ *Define your goal in terms of steps.* If you want to make better grades this six weeks, I can promise you that will be the product of lots of small steps made each and every day. It won't be some giant leap you make all at one time. Define your goal in small steps, not huge leaps.

★ *Create accountability toward the progress of your goal.* Figure out some way to hold yourself accountable for what you say you are going to do. Maybe you make the commitment to a friend and have them check on you every day or every week. Or maybe you require yourself to write down your progress every single day. Either way, make sure that you have to be accountable on a regular basis.

Nothing less than implementing these seven steps will get you what you want. Once you give yourself goals and set yourself firmly on the path of meeting them, change starts happening. Don't be fooled by all the stories you read about "overnight successes." If you really check out how they made it, you'll discover that they established their goals and went after them the same way you must go after yours: one step at a time, in which a series of smaller goals were accomplished in order to get to the big one.

YOUR SPECIFIC GOAL PLAN

What is the part of your life you need to manage the most? What do you need to work on right now to keep yourself from falling back into a

comfort zone like we talked about earlier? Reach high in setting your goals but be realistic. This is a big step in creating the plan of your life so do it thoughtfully. You've been giving up too soon and it is time to start requiring more of yourself.

I can't tell you in this book what your goals should be; only you can know that. But good life management means *specific* life management. Your goals need to be direct and clear. Let me just give you some examples:

★ **If you want more dates, then you've got to determine specific ways to better manage your social life. Set specific goals to put yourself at parties, youth groups, football games, or other activities where you have the chance of forming a relationship. Again, choose things that you can control. You can't control whether someone asks you out or not, but you can set goals to put yourself in places where you have the chance to be invited. That's what management is all about.**

★ If you want better grades, then you've got to work on "time management." Set goals to give yourself one extra hour a day for study. If you break down your day to look for that one hour as I did to pull up my grades, then you'll get results.

★ If you want to improve your personality, then determine specific ways to manage the parts of your personality that are lacking. If you think you fade into the woodwork too easily, then set specific goals to walk into a classroom, make eye contact, and speak to three people. Basically, write yourself a script. If you think your teacher is ignoring you, then set a goal to make an appointment with that teacher after school, sit down with him or her, and see if that teacher will treat you like a human being. If you think you are too sarcastic, set specific goals to say something positive to three different people a day.

★ If you want to get rid of some destructive habits—smoking, weekend drinking, casual sex, whatever—then you've got to manage your way out of them. It isn't going to be good enough to just decide to say no. There are going to be great temptations and peer pressure for you to stick with your old ways. You need to have very specific goals about how to keep yourself out of situations where the peer pressure is going to be intense. You've got to have a plan to be somewhere else on Friday nights instead of at a party with alcohol. You've got to have a specific plan to keep you from getting in the backseat with somebody so that the chance to have sex is far less likely.

THE FINISH LINE IS IN SIGHT!

Managing your life does not mean overnight changes. Changes will come slowly. But so what? There is power in persistence. The philosopher Samuel Johnson once wrote that "great acts are performed not through strength but by perseverance." And that is true; the simple small goals are what's going to transform your life.

Through our life management, as we accomplish each small goal, we will discover that we have even more goals we want to reach. We will wake up every day feeling a passion to get even more things accomplished. We will feel productive and confident in a way we never knew we could feel. We will develop far more control over our destiny. I guarantee you that goals are a great key to teach us to believe in ourselves, and with such belief, we will stay at the front of the parade.

Now, I hope that you move on to some goals that are important to you. Use programming instead of willpower, expect problems rather than moaning about them, and use project status priorities to get you going on them. These are the tools that will really help you become a better life manager than ever before.

Resolve right now to manage your life and you will find that the more you do it, the easier it gets. Managing a life that is a total wreck is a big problem and challenge. But once you get it on a roll, once you have momentum, your management starts to feed on itself and you will love the result.

LIGHTBULBS

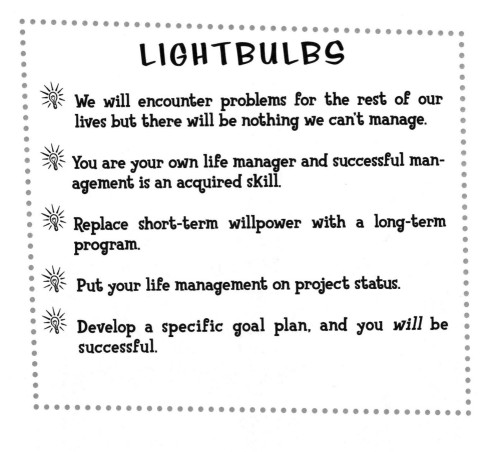

- We will encounter problems for the rest of our lives but there will be nothing we can't manage.

- You are your own life manager and successful management is an acquired skill.

- Replace short-term willpower with a long-term program.

- Put your life management on project status.

- Develop a specific goal plan, and you *will* be successful.

LIFE LAW EIGHT

WE TEACH PEOPLE HOW TO TREAT US

Don't make yourself a mouse, or the cat will eat you.

—A. B. Cheales

WHY YOU SHOULD READ THIS LIFE LAW:

To start controlling and stop complaining about your relationships. Learn to renegotiate with everyone in your life to get the treatment that you want and deserve.

SHE COULD HEAR HER DAD SNORING AND THEIR bedroom TV was off, so Jan was sure that her parents were asleep. She slipped out of the house and quietly raised the garage door. Without starting the engine, she pushed the family car out to the street.

Then, a good twenty yards from the house, Jan started the car and was gone. She was loving it. Freedom! It was midnight, and she headed to her friend Marcy's house.

For a fifteen-year-old girl, Jan knew her way around town pretty well. She had made the trip to Marcy's house at least twenty times, all of them after midnight. Her dad had once asked her if she was taking the car out when no one was around, but she had given him a very persuasive answer that she wouldn't ever do such a thing.

When she got to Marcy's, she tapped on her bedroom window. No answer. Marcy wasn't home. It was stupid not to have called, but she didn't want to wake up Marcy's parents. "Oh, well," Jan thought, "I had better return home. No harm done."

As Jan pulled up to her house, she turned off the ignition and coasted into the driveway like she always did. There, to her shock, she found her father, not asleep like he was supposed to be, but standing instead with his hand extended asking for the keys.

Jan was terrified. "Oh, God, I'm dead now," she whispered. But all her dad said was, "Go to your room."

For three days, her father said nothing. Then, the day before her sixteenth birthday, he asked Jan to take a ride with him in the car. He drove straight to the Ford dealership. Once there, her dad had a brand-new Ford Mustang brought up for Jan to test-drive. She was ecstatic. This was her dream car: a bright red convertible with a white top and a CD player.

With her dad in the passenger seat, Jan drove the Mustang up and down streets, squealing with delight, then headed back to the dealership. She and her father went into the dealer's office. Jan couldn't believe it. This was really going to happen.

Then the dealer handed Jan's father a check. "What?" Jan asked, confused.

"I'm getting a refund on the Mustang you just drove," said her dad. "It was going to be your sixteenth birthday present."

What is this story about? Is it just a story about a girl who got hammered by some very strict parents? That's what Jan thought had happened to her. For weeks, she went around school talking about how cruel her father was, how he had publicly humiliated her, how he had set up this scene at the dealership just to teach her a lesson. She was convinced her parents were really, really mean. She was completely missing what had happened.

RENEGOTIATING YOUR RELATIONSHIP

As you know from reading the previous Life Laws, people "size you up" based upon the way you present yourself to the world. Through that presentation, they are deciding what you can bring to their life and what they can bring to yours. They are deciding what they can do for you, and what you can do for them. They are deciding what they can accept from you and what you will accept from them.

In other words, they decide how to treat you. When making this decision, they will essentially test you, and based on your response to their tests, they will either continue with their initial way of treating you or they will change their approach. Do you see what this means? It means that you get to greatly influence their decisions. You can be the one who sets the tone.

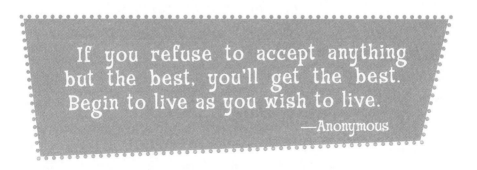

If you refuse to accept anything but the best, you'll get the best. Begin to live as you wish to live.

—Anonymous

If you reward someone's behavior by reacting in a way they desire, you are likely to see that behavior again. If you respond in a way that they find undesirable, you are less likely to see that behavior again. Don't kid yourself; this is true and it will always be true, with almost everybody you encounter.

It even applies to your enemies, particularly when you both occupy the same rung on the social ladder. If someone at school is continually taking unfair potshots at you, you are somehow rewarding that behavior—otherwise, that person wouldn't be so likely to continue it. If someone at school is trying to continually hurt you by excluding you from a certain group or an activity, you are somehow rewarding that behavior, however unintentionally, or that person wouldn't continue it.

In reality you have somehow communicated, by word or deed, and taught that person that his or her behavior is acceptable to you. That means you must own, rather than complain about, how people treat you.

For you and me as young people, this is a great Life Law for us to understand because it truly teaches us how to greatly influence key situations in our lives. Please know that for the vast majority of you, I'm including your parents in this equation. I know that a lot of you say that you simply don't have control or even any influence over your life. You feel like you don't have control because you live with your parents and they decide what you get to do, when you get to do it, who you get to do it with; they get to decide everything. But that is only true to an extent. Just like Jan, the girl who lost her Mustang, you clearly have at least some control over what your parents do.

Because parents are the people we encounter most frequently and also the people who now have the most control over our lives, I'm going to focus primarily on parents in this chapter. Even if our parents set boundaries and limits that we have to follow, we can have an influence over what those boundaries are. Sometimes, if we are smart, we can get them to widen the boundaries within which we operate—all because we teach them how to treat us.

Before we go any further into Life Law Eight, I want to make sure that we have the same understanding as to what a typical interaction with your parents is like.

* Do you feel like your parents don't listen to a word you say?
* Do you ever want to remind your parents that your third birthday was a long time ago so they will quit treating you like a toddler?
* Do your parents give you a long lecture including a list of "you should've . . ." while you're thinking "I could've . . . but I didn't"?
* Do your parents give you a history lesson about when they were teenagers that is so boring you're thinking of marketing it as a lullaby?
* Do you bring up a problem of yours, and your parents so often try to top it with a problem of theirs that you're thinking of bringing up world hunger and nuclear warfare next time?
* Do you ever feel that your parents are convinced that you have three remaining brain cells, and they are fighting?
* Do your parents pass out more advice than Dr. Drew and Adam Carolla on *Loveline?*

If you could relate with any of the above take a look at the typical postinteraction reactions. Then see if you have these reactions after a parental encounter:

- ★ You feel totally ignored.
- ★ You feel put down and condescended to.
- ★ You feel so sick of being told what to do that you could scream so loud that glass in Antarctica would shatter.
- ★ You feel that you may actually go crazy.
- ★ You feel angry and frustrated.
- ★ You feel more controlled than airport traffic.
- ★ You feel hurt.

So there's usually a standoff. You become frustrated and resigned to the fact that your parents are tyrannical controllers rather than thinking and feeling people. You figure there is nothing you can do to get your parents to see you as a young adult rather than a totally dependent child.

But here's the only question on the table: Even if your parents are being unreasonable, what are you going to do to change the way they treat you? You taught them how to treat you. Now all you have to do is teach them to treat you a different way.

RED ALERT!

Stop! Hold on! Time out! I need to clarify a huge exception to this law. This law only works if the people with whom you are dealing are not sicko freaks who need therapy or worse.

You are, for absolute sure, entitled to be treated with dignity and respect. If someone is rude or inconsiderate, that's one thing. If they are physically, mentally, or emotionally abusing you, that's totally different. You did not teach them to do that!

If you are being sexually molested, raped, or parentally neglected, *it is not your fault! Repeat, it is not your fault!* You don't own that problem, you didn't set it up that way, and you may need help to change it or escape from it.

If any of these horrible realities are in your life, don't try to get in the bad guy's face by yourself; get help. You can do so confidentially without exposing yourself to danger. Teachers, pastors, counselors, and other trusted adults will help.

You may be trapped and you may be in danger, but others will listen and intervene only when you feel ready and confident enough to act. But you must reach out and not continue to suffer in a terrible and lonely silence.

Be there for yourself. You are worth it! Here are some numbers you can call for help.

Rape	1-800-656-4673	Rape, Abuse, and Incest National Network (RAIN)
Abuse and Neglect	1-800-422-4453	Childhelp National Child Abuse Hotline
Violence	1-800-799-7233	National Domestic Violence Hotline
Suicide	1-888-793-4357	Crisis Helpline

UPSTREAM MANAGEMENT

(So with the understanding that we are talking about parents who may be tuned out and insensitive but not sicko freaks, let's continue.) When I say that you taught them how to treat you, I mean that you train them with your reactions in the same way you train your dog to sit or roll over. Think about it; every time you and your parents interact, you respond in some way. Your response powerfully influences whether the reaction you got from your parents will repeat itself in the future or not. If, for example, you reach out to your mother by wanting to share a problem with her and she half ignores you because she is watching TV, and you just shrug your shoulders and walk off, then you have rewarded her by withdrawing and eliminating the demand that you were placing on her. In sum, you have just taught her that if she will just ignore you, you will go away.

If your parents tell you something you don't want to hear, and you blow up, yell, scream, stomp off to your room, and slam the door, then you have rewarded their strictness by reinforcing their perception of you as childlike and immature. Once again, you ended the interaction and let them off the hook.

You may also be teaching them how to treat you because you come to them only when you have some ridiculous question or problem that they have no option but to dismiss or discipline you for—questions like "Can I quit school and join a gang?" or "Can you spot me some beer money?" When you act like this, again you have taught them to deepen their perception of you as an irresponsible individual.

You can also teach people how to treat you by what you don't say. For example, you have been out with your friends and come in, however reluctantly, fifteen seconds before curfew and go straight to the refrigerator or to your room to get on the phone. Your parents track you down and the conversation goes something like:

Parent: Well, it's about time you got home, do you just sit outside until the clock ticks right down to the limit?

You: Hey, I got home on time, what do you want?

Parent: What did you do tonight?

You: Nothing.

Parent: Where did you go?

You: Nowhere.

Parent: Who were you with?

You: Nobody.

Parent: Did you have a good time?

You: I did until I had to come home before everybody else, thank you very much.

Parent: Are you going to stay on the phone all night?

You: Probably. Why?

Parent: Never mind. Good night.

Sound familiar? Here you have taught them to be nervous, really nervous, about what you are doing when you are out. People who have nothing to hide, hide nothing. You just taught them that you must have something to hide and therefore they should be nervous.

As much as that bites, you know it's true. So now let's just move on to getting them to stop treating you like a total moron. Let's move on to getting them to treat you how you should be treated. But remember, they are your parents, not your friends from school, so they will never treat you the same as your friends do; but it can get much better. It can get to a point where you can talk to your parents and get them to relate to you on a more adult-to-adult level, as opposed to always wanting to discipline you or just disregarding what you are saying.

So what we are going to do is called "upstream management." It is the old tail-wagging-the-dog story. You may not be the one in power or control, but you have significant ability to get your parents to do more of what you want them to do, and less of what you don't want them to do. All you have to do is change some key actions and reactions that you throw out there.

Change the way in which you are engaging your parents, and they will change the way they react. If you interact with your parents in any of the following ways it will greatly increase the amount of freedom and respect they give you.

Behaving Your Way to a New Relationship

1. Initiate conversations with your parents.
2. Remember, they are your parents so they will discipline you sometimes.
3. Don't take the bait; stay calm.
4. Become interested in your parents' lives and they will be interested in your life.
5. Be realistic about what you expect your parents' reactions to be.
6. Stop demanding and start earning your freedom.
7. Inspire confidence and trust through predictability.
8. Allow yourself to be influenced by your parents' advice.
9. Be easy to get along with.
10. Do not talk to your parents only when you have a problem, because if all you talk about are problems, that is a problem.

I WASN'T EXPECTING YOU

Keep in mind that if your parents are resistant at first, it is because you taught them how to be. You taught them really well and now they have formed habits. Habits can be stubborn but they can change. Keep trying; this will work. Any time a relationship has gone on for months or years, both sides form the habits or expectations. You have come to expect your parents to respond in certain ways, and they have come to expect you to respond and behave in certain ways. The problem is on both ends. First and foremost, you tend to see what you are looking for. If you expect either of your parents to be negative, critical, and resistant to your ideas, that is most likely how you will interpret their behavior, even if that is not how they are actually behaving. Second, we tend to conform to that which is expected of us. In other words, if they expect you to be a knothead, throw a tantrum, and be disrespectful, there is a tendency for the two of you to define your relationship in just that way.

To make sure that you are delivering the message that you want and receiving what is actually being sent, you must check your expectations and figure out if you and your parents are setting yourselves and each other up for disaster. Realize that through your behavior you can create new expectations with your parents that get you what you want.

EXPECT ME AT ONE

When I was in high school, some of my friends were frustrated about and couldn't understand why my parents gave me more freedoms than theirs gave them, and how I got in trouble less often than they did. The reason I was allowed more freedom is because this is one of the laws that sunk in when I was still in high school. I understood that I was teaching my parents how to treat me, that I was creating expectations that created more freedom for myself. I couldn't have labeled it like that, but I did know that I was teaching them how to treat me. I had heard my dad say a million times that results are the only things that mattered, that we can only judge our life based on results. I understood that my parents would determine the amount of freedom they gave me based on the results that I gave them. So I was careful to give my parents results that demonstrated accountability, maturity, and the ability to handle freedom responsibly. In short, I was predictable. I went where

I said, did what I said, and came home when I said. As a result, I got permission to do much more than I would have *ever* been able to sneak around and do.

FREEDOMS

People learn by the results that you choose to give them, and in that respect, you are in control of every relationship you have. When my parents went out on a limb, let me do something further into the world of independence, I handled it well and did what I said I was going to do, thereby setting me up for the next freedom. It was like stepping-stones across a river. Every time I stood on one stone and didn't fall off, I could toss another one a little farther into the stream and hop onto it. Pretty soon, I had the freedom that I really wanted.

So what have you been teaching your parents? Have you been teaching them that you are reliable, predictable, and competent, or have you been teaching them that you are going to break and run off every time you get half a chance? Seriously decide what you have been doing to set your relationship up however it is, and remember, you are not a victim.

I had a friend in high school who was a perfect example of how not to earn more freedom. To say that Jason did stupid things would be a compliment. Because, let me tell you, he almost didn't even get Life Law Eight. The very day that he got his car, he decided "I am free."

He decided: "I got a car and I don't have to come home; I don't have to call home. I don't have to tell my parents what I am doing. I don't have to do squat. I finally got me a car." He left on Friday afternoon after school in his newfound freedom, aka the Jeep, and hit the town. He spent the night out and didn't call home, didn't tell his parents where he was going, didn't tell them what he was doing. He was just his own man come Friday afternoon at 3:30. When he finally did come home late Saturday afternoon—only to get a change of clothes, I might add—guess what happened? Well, big surprise, his dad took his keys away from him.

Now, you are probably thinking, "Jay, you just made that up to make a point." I wish I had, but I did not. I hated this because Jason was the oldest of our group of friends, and that meant that the rest of us lost his car, too. By not handling his new freedom that came with having his own car with maturity and discipline, by not coming home when he said he was going to come home, by not calling when he should have called, he taught his father "You have to give me a curfew. You have to give me strict rules and guidelines. You have to keep me on a very tight leash." He told his dad with his actions "I am not going to do what I should do. I am not going to do what you want me to do. So you have to make me do it. You have to give me strict rules and make me do the things that I am supposed to because I am telling you right now with my actions, I am not going to do it otherwise." That is what his dad did. He took away his car for a month and gave him an 11:30 curfew.

WHY DO THEY DO THIS?

Just like Jason, you, too, are responsible for the way that your parents are treating you. You are either teaching or allowing your parents to behave and react to you the way they do. (Remember I am talking about non-sicko parents.) You do this by choosing how to treat them. If your parents won't listen to you and don't talk to you and don't respect you as a mature individual, it may well be because:

- ★ You are totally selfish and don't listen to them either.
- ★ You ask questions and make declarations that are guaranteed to warrant resistance and negative reactions: Can I get a tattoo? Start smoking? Do drugs? Or just quit going to school? (What the hell do you expect them to say?)
- ★ You get furious if you don't get the answer that you were looking for and immediately decide your parents are enemies.
- ★ You demand rather than command the respect of your parents.

Regardless of the actual reason your parents treat you in a way that you don't like, you greatly influence that treatment.

That is both good news and bad news. It is obviously bad news because it means that we are accountable and responsible for so much of what everybody does to us and that is a big burden. It is good news because that means that we are in a position of influence. If you are unhappy, you can change it all by yourself; you don't need active help and cooperation from anyone else. You can begin making huge changes in all of your relationships completely by yourself. Simply by deciding that you will no longer accept behavior that you do not want, you are making an important commitment to change.

So how do you improve the way your parents treat you?

WHAT TO DO

Let's take a look at the Behaving Your Way to a New Relationship list we looked at earlier. Review each item and ask yourself how you can incorporate each of these points into your interaction patterns with one or both of your parents. What do you suppose it would mean to your mother and father, for example, if you simply approached them just to ask about their day, when you didn't want anything, didn't need anything, and didn't have a problem to solve? How do you suppose it would make them feel when they walked away knowing that you took an active interest in their lives? That would probably cause them to treat you like the adult you were being.

Again, include each of these points in your interactions with people, along with some patience, and I think you will be amazed at the immediate changes you can create in your relationship with your parents.

IT IS DARK INSIDE THOSE LOCKERS

Your power and ability to change relationships is not limited just to that relationship you have with your parents. You may be just as frustrated with that Neanderthal at school with the "Mama didn't love me" tattoo on his biceps who keeps picking on you. You are sick of him stuffing you in a locker, or stealing all of your lunch money, or just making an ass of you when everybody is looking. Or maybe you are sick of that walking gossip column with a ponytail telling lies about

you every time you turn your back. Well, good news—just as in the relationship with your parents, you have tremendous power and influence in this situation as well. You can change it today. You can change it because, once again, we teach people how to treat us; they don't decide on their own. Once you understand and begin to use this Life Law, your life will change for the better, and I mean immediately.

Even though you may not currently see how, or believe that you can change the way others treat you, make the decision right now that you will not give up and accept treatment that you don't want. You do have control; you do teach people how to treat you.

Remember, you are not a victim, so find your ownership. I promise you it is there, and once you find it, the power to change is yours. Your job is to find out what "payoffs" you are creating that maintain the behaviors you don't like in others. Remember from Life Law Three: For any repetitive behavior there are payoffs; and in relationships, you control the payoffs. For that reason, you are in control of every relationship you have.

YOU CAN TEACH AN OLD DOG NEW TRICKS

Don't think: "Dang! I figured this out too late. My relationships with people like my parents and certain friends are so set in stone that I am screwed forever." That is absolutely not true. All relationships can be renegotiated. You can reopen negotiations by either word or act. To do this you have to identify what you are doing to support and allow the behaviors that you don't like in others. Once you have identified those, then you start changing to make them change, and people will treat you in a different way.

Of course, you know there will be resistance. Anytime you change your relationship in a way that requires more of the other person or takes away something that they used to enjoy, there will be resistance. But there will also be some resistance within yourself. One of the strange laws of human nature is that we tend to conform to that which is expected of us. In other words, if you are a jock and people expect you to do poorly in class, you tend not to study because people don't anticipate you making an A. If you're the class clown, you know how difficult it is not to act funny when a lot of people expect you to be that way. Or it's hard not to act like the stone-cold macho man if that's what other students expect of you.

I have saved one of the most important concepts for last because I want it to be fresh in your mind and stand out above all else. The most important relationship you will ever have, and the one that sets the tone for every other relationship in your life, is the relationship that you have with yourself. Everyone in your life will watch how you treat you, what you require of you, and whether or not you are willing to stand up for you. When you treat yourself with dignity and respect, you send a loud and clear message that you are now in a position of strength and power. You are sending a loud and clear message to better negotiate what you really want. You are in a better position to renegotiate how people treat you.

> It is not fair to ask others what you are not willing to do yourself.
> —Eleanor Roosevelt

From this position, you can teach people to perceive and treat you in the way that you feel you actually should be perceived and treated. If you do not have the conviction in your heart and mind as to who and what you are and what you require, you will always be creating more problems than you could ever imagine. You'll be letting people in your life who are not particularly interested in treating you with dignity and respect. You'll let people in your life who will treat you on less than a quality level. You'll let people into your life who will try to make you feel guilty, who will want to manipulate you, who will turn on you whenever the pressure is on.

Ultimately, remember the principle of reciprocity: You get what you give. You should never expect people to give you something you are unwilling to give yourself.

LIGHTBULBS

☼ People "size you up" based on how you present yourself to the world.

☼ People then test you to see how you allow them to treat you.

☼ You can control your life by working within the boundaries that you are limited by. You can reteach people how to treat you.

☼ Treat yourself well so others will be motivated to do the same.

LIFE LAW NINE

THERE IS POWER IN FORGIVENESS

Man is free at the moment he wishes to be.

—Voltaire

To set yourself free of the anger, hatred, and bitterness that result from bad treatment. Learn to exercise the choice of forgiveness.

M Y LIFELONG FRIEND MATT AND I USED TO RIDE four-wheelers all through some wooded areas near our houses. We would literally ride for hours until the engines were so hot they were just glowing. One day I stupidly reached into Matt's four-wheeler to pull out a branch that had become lodged between the engine and frame and just seared the back of my hand. In that split-second that my hand was up against that hot metal, it hurt, and it hurt plenty. But when I jerked my hand away, the hurting didn't stop. I had been severely burned, and the pain lasted for days and days, long after the actual burning was over.

The very same thing happens when someone hurts you emotionally. The pain lasts long after the actual event. It can go on for days, weeks, months, even years. It can diminish your confidence, your self-esteem, and possibly change your heart and make you bitter.

I'll bet one thing that you and I can agree on is that being a teenager means that you have lots of experience at getting jerked around. Let's face it: At this stage of life, there are lots of people above you in the pecking order, and they aren't very sensitive to what you think and feel. There are a lot of people who see life as a fierce contest in which they always want to "one up" you, even if it means backstabbing you. They make you the target of lies, gossip, and other mean and hateful attacks with words. They hurt you by isolating you and leaving you out of activities you want and deserve to participate in.

You may also have parents who have mistreated you in some way, unfairly punishing you or perhaps even horribly or criminally abusing you. It may be that teachers have blamed you for things you didn't do or have held you up to ridicule. You no doubt have been wronged by any number of things, and you have justifiable reasons to be angry, hateful, resentful, or bitter. "Look at what people have done to me," you want to say. "They've been mean and cruel. I've been falsely accused, blamed for things I didn't even know about, wounded by hateful lies about what I did or did not do."

And let's be honest. When people criticize you, gossip about you, yell at you, or even physically hurt you, it's very difficult to let it go. It's hard not to hold a grudge.

But here's the decision you have to make: Do you want to think you're right, or do you want to be happy? Do you want to be a martyr? Or do you want to stop being mad every day?

It's a strange question, isn't it? But I'll try to explain.

OUCH AND RE-OUCH!

When something or someone hurts you, it is only natural that you would have a negative reaction. Anger is a normal human emotion. So is hurt. It not only causes an ouch, but there is a re-ouch to the original ouch. A girl by the name of Kacey, a soon-to-be college freshman, told me this story about her experience with a re-ouch.

"When I was in the seventh grade, there was this boy I adored. I had the biggest crush on him. Then I heard him telling his friends that he thought I was a fat and ugly monster. I was walking right by him, and he just said that as if he knew I would hear it. It was awful." And here Kacey was six years later, still talking about the humiliation of that day.

Hurt, hate, anger, frustration, and bitterness are some of the most powerful experiences you'll have. They are so powerful that when they are present, they absolutely change who you are and push all other feelings and emotions into the background. Think about a time in your life when someone said something truly ugly about you. Didn't that hurt go on for a long time?

If you really get hurt, and if you get hurt often enough, then you'll start withdrawing emotionally. You'll withdraw one of three ways:

1. You'll live behind an emotional safety wall, keeping yourself away from others so they can't hurt you again. You simply won't let yourself care or feel. You'll get emotional when you read a book or watch a sad movie, maybe, but you're too scared to take the real-life risk of needing or wanting anyone to like you or care about or share with you.

2. You'll turn sullen and sarcastic, becoming a master of the put-down, thinking that it's better to get others before they get you. Your thinking is that if you can reject people first, then you won't be as wounded if they reject you. You rationalize by saying, "I didn't like them anyway. I pushed them away from me, so it was my choice, not theirs."

3. You'll become a robot and just won't acknowledge feelings, good or bad. You're not just withdrawn, you become remote. People ask you if you're paying attention, if you even know where you are. Your theory to life becomes: "If I don't care, I don't hurt. If I don't want, I don't lose."

Moreover, carrying fear, frustration, disappointment, and anger within you changes your physical being. It creates a physical imbalance where you have too much of some things and not enough of others. You may be experiencing sleep disturbance, nightmares, poor concentration, and fatigue. You may have tension headaches, migraine headaches, ulcers, acne, back spasms. Such pain can even cause you to have a heart attack at your young age. You may experience nervousness, never having a peaceful moment because you are constantly upset. That is not okay. It is not okay to settle for a silent, private hell. Don't settle for such an existence just because you don't feel worthy of causing a problem or drawing attention to yourself. Just as you cannot be happy and sad at the same time, you cannot be peaceful and in turmoil at the same time. You cannot have hope and optimism while you are withdrawn and shut down. You cannot be physically calm and constantly nervous at the same time. However you try to set up your protection, holding on to such anger and pain and resentment exacts a very high price from you.

Why stay trapped in a lonely dark prison, where it is impossible for happiness, hope, and optimism to grow? Within that prison, you might fly into rages where you fight back, or you'll withdraw emotionally, curling up, hoping that the hurt will go away. You can justify your misery because it was caused by the action of someone else, but really, what kind of life is it for you? As long as you are nursing that misery, you aren't functioning at your peak. You are still letting that person hurt you. Regardless of how that person initially hurt you, you're letting him or her cause you still greater pain.

I recently experienced a tragic example of this. The following is a letter I received on just this subject.

> Be your own palace or the world's your jail.
>
> —Anonymous

Dear Jay:

I was a participant in your focus group last week to help contribute ideas and topics for your book. I was quiet last week; but I had a lot to say. You talked a lot about the power in forgiveness to free yourself from an emotional prison with someone. I can painfully relate with what you said.

For a period that lasted exactly a year and 4 months and 8 days, I was molested and eventually raped by my stepfather. It began the night of my 13th birthday when he came to sit on the edge of my bed to tell me he was glad I was finally a woman. He began to touch me in ways that made me wish mom hadn't already gone to bed.

He returned night after night, and eventually sitting on the edge of the bed turned into sitting on the bed, sitting in the bed, then lying in the bed, then claiming and taking the bed and myself as his own.

I never told my mom, he said if I did they would break up and it would be my fault, not his. He made mom so happy I didn't dare say a word. I didn't know better.

They finally divorced for unrelated reasons and I was set free from my physical prison in my bed; but I have remained in my emotional prison for four years since. I've withdrawn myself from my life. I went from pretty and popular to seemingly ugly and terrified of boys.

Although this monster is no longer physically in my life, his memories still haunt me. I think of what he did to me everyday. It is my first thought in the morning and my last thought at night. I feel dirty, ugly, and damaged, and I am afraid to date. I don't know what to do.

Sincerely

Mindy

Mindy was a victim, plain and simple, too young to protect herself, too confused to assert herself, too afraid to reach out for help. What happened to her was not fair; it was not explainable and there was no way to make sense of it. She should not have had to deal with such a horrific event. It should not have taken anything away from the life of this wonderful girl. Nonetheless, it was there—and fair or unfair, it was her burden.

BREAKING THE BONDS OF HATRED AND PAIN

Obviously, Mindy had chosen to react to the abuse by becoming withdrawn and shut down. It was hard to fault her. But Mindy did have another choice, a proactive choice. She could have chosen instead to say, "As unfair as this is, I will deal with it. Instead of shutting down for the rest of my life, I can break out of this prison and reclaim a place in the world. I may have a right to be bitter and angry but I have a responsibility not to be."

Breaking out and reclaiming her place in the fully functioning world would, of course, be the better choice for Mindy. Not necessarily the easy choice, but the better one. As long as she is filled with bitterness toward her ex-stepfather, she is locked in a bond with him that will absolutely kill her spirit. It is bad enough that he did those horrible things to her for over a year. Now, four years later, he is still poisoning her life. He is still hurting her day after day after day by poisoning the way she sees the world, and herself. He is poisoning every relationship she might ever have and enjoy. She

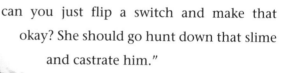
has chosen to give him the power to dominate her. She is truly locked in an emotional prison and, unfortunately, that prison door locks from the inside. Only she can let herself out and dictate her own life.

That's a tough thing for me to say. I wish there were some magic words I could pass on to her that would change her life and make her better. But she has to do it. That's the way the world works. Although she is not responsible for what happened to her or the hurt that resulted from it, she has to be responsible for handling it. And what I'm about to say is going to sound even tougher, but here goes:

The way she has to handle it is that she must find the strength to forgive him. She has got to make the choice of saying, "I will not hate you another day. I will not invest my spirit in you another day. I will not remain locked in this sick bond with you another day. I will forgive you so I can be free."

"Now wait just a damn minute," you may be thinking. "How can you forgive a sick animal who has done something like that to you? How can you just flip a switch and make that okay? She should go hunt down that slime and castrate him."

Hey, castration with a dull hacksaw is probably too good for him. And Mindy ought to do whatever it takes to get him held accountable. Maybe she should contact the authorities; file a complaint; have him arrested, convicted, and put in jail for as long as the law allows. If it ruins his life, tough. I personally hope it does, but whether she does that or whether she doesn't, that isn't the ultimate step that she must take to get him in the past and out of her heart and mind. Jail will not keep him from emotionally poisoning her life.

Ultimately, she cannot be free until she makes the choice and decision to forgive him.

WHAT IS FORGIVENESS?

Now, let's make sure we're on the same page here. Anger is a fact of life. It is an emotion that should not be stifled. If you have been wronged, you should feel wronged and you should say so. It's important that you correct someone who needs correcting. But then it's important to do one other thing: to let the anger go.

All the world's great religions try to inspire their followers not to hold grudges, not to take revenge, not to mistreat someone who has mistreated you. This isn't just a pious Sunday school thing to say. The religions of the world tell you to let God get even with the jerks in your life who have hurt you. The worst thing for you, they suggest, is to seek vengeance yourself, to spend so much time and energy occupying your brain with thoughts about your enemies.

The best thing for you is to forgive. When you forgive a person, you thrive in spite of him or her. You blossom. You realize that as good as it feels to hold a grudge and to be righteously angry, overcoming a grudge can be a much, much better feeling. As the old saying goes, "Living well is the best revenge."

Does this mean that I'm telling you to go to the person who has hurt you and say, "I forgive you"? Absolutely not. The forgiveness I am talking about is all about you and not about whoever has hurt you. I don't care if these other people ever even know that you have forgiven them. I don't care if they ever even acknowledge that they have hurt you. You are the only person who has to know about this forgiveness because this is something that takes place within you and for you.

Forgiving for Mindy does not mean going to her abusive stepfather and saying, "It's okay. All is forgiven." Forgiving simply means that she will no longer spend one more minute of one more hour of one more day allowing her heart to be dominated by these negative emotions about him. She should forgive him not as a gift to him but as a gift to herself.

Perhaps you've not had as painful a past as Mindy. Nonetheless, aren't you, too, carrying great burdens? With you, the perpetrators might be parents, teachers, friends, girlfriends or boyfriends, or some other person in your life. But regardless of the degree of severity, don't you, too, have the same challenge as Mindy? Aren't you confronted with the same choices she is? As unfair as it is for you to have to be carrying the burden of being wronged by someone else, don't you, too, have a choice to make? Will you continue to carry the burden and the dark and bitter feelings that come with that burden, or will you break out of your personal prison and reclaim your place in the world of happy people?

★   Is it fair that you got put in this prison? No.

★   Is it easy to get out of it? No.

★   Is it worth it? Yes. You bet it is—because you are worth it.

If you forgive the person who has hurt you, stolen your boyfriend or girlfriend away, or gossiped about you, you are saying essentially to that person, "I will no longer suffer 24/7 because you are a jerk. I'm not going to get filled up with hate when I pass by you in the hall. I'm not going to shut down emotionally anymore, with my teeth gritting and the blood boiling in my forehead."

> Forgive your enemies, but never forget their names.
>
> —John Fitzgerald Kennedy

If you think, "Nice advice, Jay, but I'm still pissed off at Jane or John or Mom or Dad or whoever," then I need to remind you of one thing. The world doesn't care that you are pissed. You can sit up in your room every night angry, bitter, and shut down and I guarantee you that won't do one thing to change what is wrong in your life. The world just keeps on spinning around. Your friends keep going on dates, everybody keeps going to the football games or the parties, everybody continues to have a good time whether you shut down or not. So understand that you are not helping yourself, and you are not getting sympathy with your suffering. The person who hurt you is probably at home in bed sleeping like a baby and you are up tormented over what he or she did to you. That is why you need to take a second look at forgiveness. Once again, forgiveness is all about you and not about the person you are forgiving. This is about you saying, "You have hurt me enough; I will not take over for you and make sure that I stay miserable by staying angry and pissed off. I am choosing to give me the gift of love."

What you want is "emotional closure." You want to be able to say honestly that you have no unfinished emotional business left with the people you have been focused on. If you have this burning need to go tell them what jerks they are and you just cannot be at peace until you have done that, then you don't have emotional closure. If every day you get up and feel the need to go over and over in your mind what they have done to you and how unfair it is, then you don't have emotional closure. It is important that you be genuine here as opposed to sarcastic. You can't say, "Hey, I forgive you and good luck to you," and then under your breath say, "God is going to fry your butt up someday." That is not forgiving. That is just changing your words of bitterness.

To be really free, you have to really forgive.

TURNING FORGIVENESS INTO ACTION

Can you do it? Can you forgive? The "how to forgive" is not easy, but it can be done. The first thing you have to understand is that forgiveness is not a feeling; it is a decision. You may have been sitting around waiting for some warm wave of forgiveness to wash over your body and give you this peaceful and still feeling. Not going to happen. Forgiveness is a decision. It is not an emotion, and believe me, that is good news. Fortunately, charitable and forgiving feelings don't have to be in place for you to free yourself from this emotional prison. Forgiveness is an intellectual choice.

What you want to aim for is what I call the "I'm out of here response"—that is, the very least that you have to do in order to get the emotional closure that we just discussed. This response is going to be different for every person in every situation. For example, if some clerk is rude to you in the store and it really makes you mad, maybe your response is simply to leave and take your business somewhere else, knowing that you will have made your statement by never returning to that store or dealing with that clerk again. If the transgression against you is much more serious like in the case of Mindy, then certainly much more is required. Maybe it's going to the police, or finally confronting him face-to-face or writing him a letter expressing her feelings, whether or not she chooses to mail it.

What you want to do is identify the least demanding thing you can do that will allow you to get emotional closure. Figure out who in your life has you locked in the tractor beam of bitterness and resentment, and then decide how to achieve emotional closure with that person.

Let's go through that process right now. Below are five steps that if followed will allow you to achieve emotional closure and thus take your power back.

1. Search your mind and heart and identify all of those people who, in your opinion, have jerked you around or hurt you in some way that has filled your heart with negative emotions. I've given five spaces below for you to list these people one by one. If there are more, list them on the side of the page.

1. ....

2. ....

3. ....

4. ....

5. ....

2.   Now describe specifically what it is they have done to you and, therefore, what you must forgive and get emotional closure on.

1. ....

2. ....

3. ....

4. ....

5. ....

3.   Now search your mind and heart and identify your "I'm out of here response" for each of these people. Do you need to confront them? Or can you handle this entirely within you? Do you need to write them a letter? Do you need to call the police? What is the least thing you can do that will allow you to say, "This is it, it is all over, I am out of here"?

1. ....

2. ....

3. ....

4. ....

5. ....

4. Now write the words you need to say to yourself to claim the freedom that comes from forgiveness.

1. ....

2. ....

3. ....

4. ....

5. ....

5. Last, take just a moment to write down how you will feel once you are free of the negative emotions that have had you locked in a bond with this person.

1. ....

2. ....

3. ....

4. ....

5. ....

GIVING WHAT YOU HAVE

There is one more thing you should remember about the power of forgiveness. You are not the only one who pays a price when anger, hatred, and bitterness dominate you. Those who love you pay a high price as well. If all of the emotions you have are negative ones due to your resentments and your grudges, then those are the only emotions you can give to others. You can't give away emotions that you don't have or that you are not nurturing. You cannot give a pure love to your girlfriend or boyfriend, or your brother or your parents, if your heart is full of anger. You can't give out quality love to people if you are shut down to protect yourself against pain. You may think you can hate your parents and still love your girlfriend or boyfriend, but you can't. Maybe you feel that you are escaping into their arms with love today, but as time wears on, deep anger will creep in and poison that relationship. Get those emotions out of there so that all that's in your heart is love, forgiveness, light, hope, and optimism.

Trust me, everyone in your life will reap great benefits from you doing this. Let's say, for instance, that you have been jerked around by the last few people you have dated. As a result, you have a terrible chip on your shoulder and don't trust the opposite sex as far as you can throw it. The next person to date you is dead in the water before he even gets started. He is going to pay for all of the sins and transgressions of those who came before him, and he hasn't even had a chance to do anything wrong yet. You are going to contaminate your relationships by the baggage you drag into them. You are going to contaminate your relationships by your inability to forgive those from your past. Because you haven't reached emotional closure with your previous boyfriends or girlfriends, you're going to let them continue to control you in your future relationships, to control every successive relationship you will ever have. If that is not an incentive to motivate you to want to be free, I don't know what is.

Bottom line: Forgive. Take your power back. You're worth it.

LIGHTBULBS

- Realize that emotional wounds scar like physical wounds.

- Remember that withdrawing emotionally can affect you physically.

- To hold on to previous hurts poisons all potential relationships.

- Forgiveness is a choice that you are entitled to.

- No matter who you are, you are worth it.

YOU HAVE TO NAME IT BEFORE YOU CAN CLAIM IT

The indispensable first step to getting the things that you want out of life is this: Decide what you want.

—Ben Stein

To get dead-on specific about what you want and find the courage to step up to what is yours.

S O HERE WE ARE, AT THE VERY LAST LIFE LAW. You now have an incredible new set of skills. Now is when you have to get absolutely clear about what you want and how you are going to use your skills to get what you want. You are probably thinking, "Jay, you want me to tell you what I want? No problem. This is just like sitting on Santa's lap. Let me rip through my list. I want a new car, cool clothes, and a cell phone. I want to be in love with the best-looking guy or girl at school. I want to be famous. I want to be a star. I want my parents to give me more money. I want to have lots of fun every Friday night."

Wait a second. That's not what I'm asking you. Cars get old, clothes go out of style, cell phones cut off half the time, and dates get goofy. I'm not talking about stuff. I want to know what you really want.

"Okay, great, Jay, I get it. You want the beauty-pageant kind of answer. Okay, I want world peace; I want to wipe out hunger, save the whales and the rainforests. Basically, I want to be happy! Next Question."

Nice answer, but you probably don't know what that truly means. You say you want to be happy? Hey, my dog, Barkley, wants to be happy. Does that mean that you and my dog want the same thing? I don't think so, unless your definition of happiness means someone scratching your belly and letting you sleep under the coffee table.

When you say you want to be happy and successful, do you know precisely what that means? Do you know precisely what you want your life to be? Because you've got to be drop-dead, bull's-eye, dead-on sure of what you want, or you might blow right by it and not even know it's there. You've got to know everything about it. You've got to know how it looks, feels, smells—everything. So let me ask you again: Are you able to describe specifically what it is that you value for your life and are you willing to work toward that? Can you stand up right now and declare what you want? Can you tell me the very thing you need to feel completely fulfilled? Can you name it? Think hard. If you were walking down the street and you found a genie in a bottle, and you had just one wish, would you know what to ask for? Do you know exactly what to say? Or would you be like the guy who wished for a million bucks but mispronounced it and ended up with a shitload of ducks?

Winners in life are those who know exactly what they want. They can visualize themselves at that place where they are perfectly happy. They know exactly what they are going to have and who's going to be there when they have it. It's as simple as that. Happy people generally know what they want and feel that they are moving in the direction of getting it. That's what makes them happy. They feel that they are headed for something they love.

If you don't know what you want—if you don't know where you are going or what you are working toward—

how are you ever going to figure out how to get there? How will you ever know which choices to make and which actions to take?

Although it's easy to complain about what we don't want, it is surprisingly difficult to say what we do want. It's time you fix that.

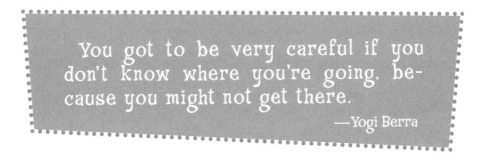

You got to be very careful if you don't know where you're going, because you might not get there.

—Yogi Berra

MAKE A PLAN, STAN

You may be saying, "Jay, if this is so important, why did you wait until the end to tell us about it?" The fact is that before you started this book, you probably didn't have much of a chance of accomplishing your goals even if you did know what they were. But now that you have done the work and are therefore among those who "get it," you're ready to put the other Life Laws into effect and aim them at a target that defines you in this world.

But make no mistake. You have to do it.

And that means you have to have a clear image of what you want your life to look like at its best. You need to know exactly how you want your ideal life to be. You want to know so that every step you take from now on helps you get to that destiny.

I promise you, I didn't know what I wanted. I could not for the life of me come up with something that seemed to fill the bill. And when I started trying to figure it out, I made some big mistakes. I would decide I wanted one thing one day and then wake up and change my mind and want another thing the next day.

A lot of people spend their whole lives acting like this. They are totally convinced they know what they want and work years and years to get there, and when they finally do, they realize that it wasn't what they really wanted at all. They had been moving in the wrong direction and wasting all that precious effort. Had they taken the time to genuinely figure things out, had they been moving down the right road instead of the wrong road, their lives would be completely different.

You will have a great advantage in life if you learn how to name it accurately before you claim it. So don't take lightly the step of defining your dream. It deserves all of your attention, all of your urgency. You want to be flexible and study all your options. But don't be lazy and tell yourself that your "dreams" should not be taken seriously. Just as you know that you have to sign up in time for cheerleader or football team tryouts, you have to name what you want because people won't wait on you to make up your mind.

I'LL TAKE DOOR #3 . . . NO, DOOR #2 . . . NO, DOOR #1 . . .

Let me give you a huge tip here. I want to tell you about the biggest mistake that I made in defining my goals—a mistake I have since learned is the single biggest screwup people make when determining what they want in life. So read the following with both eyes and your full attention. Here it is:

Don't become fixated on some object, event, or activity as the thing that you want, when in reality what you want is the feeling you think that object, event, or activity will give you!

Totally confusing, right? Let me painfully explain.

Just before my sixteenth birthday, I decided that I needed something. I had my permit and had passed my driver's test. Now I needed *a car.* And I can be persistent, real persistent. My dad calls it "perseverating," and I shifted into high gear. I bugged my parents morning, noon, and night. And as I kept reminding them, I did have a birthday coming up. To make this long story longer, I got the car. I was thrilled. I kept telling my parents that the car was exactly what I had wanted to make my life right.

I had the car for two years and I absolutely loved it. But, and this is a huge BUT, it didn't take long for me to realize that the reason I loved that car didn't have one thing to do with what I really "wanted" for my life. What's obvious in hindsight is that what I really wanted was the freedom and popularity that came with having my own car.

Mistaking what you really want can be an incredibly devastating problem if the item you become fixated on is unattainable. Let's take a really weird example. If you decide that the only thing that can make you happy is to be friends with Michael Jordan or Claudia Schiffer, the chances are it's not going to happen. And if you remain fixated on that desire, then you can spend your whole life being frustrated, because what you think you want, you know you're not going to get.

But what did you really want in that instance? The truth of the matter is that you probably wanted to have the feelings that come from being friends with Michael Jordan or Claudia Schiffer. What you wanted was simply to feel special and accepted in the eyes of someone you respect.

GO FOR THE FEELINGS AND EXPERIENCES, NOT THE THINGS

By refusing to become fixated on an object, event, or activity as the focus of what you "want," you give yourself a lot of flexibility. If you are wise enough to realize that what you want are the feelings you think would come from getting a car or being friends with a superstar, then you can find any number of ways to get that feeling. If you are open to different experiences, you may find, for example, that you get real feelings of self-respect and pride from being a good friend rather than from having a superstar friend. Or, as in the case with me and the car, you may find that there are hundreds of ways to feel like you have no freedom or to feel more popular that have nothing to do with what you drive, or what you wear. Admittedly, if you are going to pursue the wrong goal, a new car is a pretty good "wrong goal," but it's wrong nonetheless.

THE NAME GAME

Based on what I learned from my own mistakes, I was able to help a participant in one of the focus groups I conducted during the research for this book. Like me, Nick had locked in on a specific object and event as what he wanted rather than focusing on feelings and experiences. Nick was absolutely a star in everything that he did. He was a lights-out star on the basketball team and he was brilliant in the classroom. Coaches loved him, teachers loved him, and every parent wished that he was their son. Everybody considered him funny, laid-back, and easy to be with, the kind of guy who could help you with your jump shot and your homework.

Nick also came from a pretty good gene pool. For starters, his dad was a rocket scientist, and I don't mean that as a figure of speech. He was literally a rocket scientist. His sister had graduated from high school the year before Nick started with a straight-A average and a scholarship to Harvard. Talk about a hard act to follow.

And apparently, Nick was feeling the pressure. He told the group that what he really wanted for his high school years had been to make the honor roll every year so that he would win a particular award during his high school graduation ceremony. The problem is, the third trimester of his freshman year, he missed the honor roll by one-tenth of one point, disqualifying him for the award. I was sitting there thinking, "I would have killed for this guy's grade-point average." But this wasn't about me; it was about Nick. He was devastated. He said, "Now no matter what I do, no matter how hard I work, I cannot win that award, so I am screwed."

I decided it was time to do with Nick what I should have done with myself when I was in high school. I had to get him to realize that what he wanted was not some $1.98 pin he'd receive at an awards ceremony three years down the road, but instead what he wanted was the feeling that he thought the pin would bring him. I videotaped the focus group. Here's an excerpt from our conversation:

Jay: So, Nick, what is it that you really wanted?

Nick: I wanted that pin at the graduation ceremony so everyone would know that I wasn't the idiot in the family.

Jay: So what are you going to have to do to get the pin?

Nick: You are not listening; that is over. I cannot get the pin because you have to make honor roll every trimester for four years and I missed it.

Jay: So how would the pin have made you feel? How would it have felt to walk across the stage and get the pin in front of your family and all of your friends?

Nick: It would have felt great. I wouldn't have walked across that stage; I would have strutted across that stage. I can't tell you how proud I would have felt to walk across that stage getting recognized for my brains instead of my jump shot.

Jay: So what you really want is to feel proud of yourself for your brains and academic achievement, right?

Nick: Yeah, right. That is what I said.

Jay: So what are you going to have to do to feel proud of yourself?

Nick: Hell, I don't know. I can't get the pin, so I guess just do good in all the rest of the trimesters and hope I get a good class rank and go to a good school.

Jay: So how would you feel if you really worked hard, did your best, got a great ranking in the class, and went to a really good college somewhere when the time came?

Nick: Well, I would be proud of that. I would feel like I had achieved something that I could respect myself for.

Jay: So what you really want is to feel self-respect and pride in your achievements, isn't that right?

Nick: Yeah, that's right.

Jay: And that doesn't have anything to do with a pin, does it? That pin doesn't make you smart; you make you smart.

Nick: So I guess your point is, maybe my life is not totally over?

Nick laughed—he got the point. I hope you get it as well. You have to be flexible and you have to be specific. Don't ever think because one goal or plan falls by the wayside or becomes unattainable that the window of opportunity is closed and that you are transmuted into some loser. Remember what you learned in Life Law Two. You create your own experience and if it doesn't work out one way, it can and will work out another.

Here is the pattern of questions I used in talking to Nick. Maybe this simple drill will help you refine your ability to name what you truly want:

1. **What do you want?**

2. **What must you do to have it?**

3. **How would you feel when you had it?**

4. **Now tell me what you really want again, but use the answer you just gave to question three. "What I really want is . . . [answer to question three]."**

5. **What must you do to have what you really want?**

6. **How would that make you feel?**

7. **Now tell me what you really want again, but use the answer you just gave to question six. "What I really want is . . . [answer to question six]."**

8. **Repeat questions four through seven as many times as necessary until the answer is certain to you.**

When you are answering these questions, be honest, be sincere, but most of all, be precise. When I say precise, I mean to be sure to describe what you want in many different ways. Be able to describe how it will look and feel. The more you know about your true goal for your life, the easier you will be able to recognize if you are taking a step in a wrong direction. You will be able to recognize if you are no longer working toward your dreams but are instead getting off track.

To give you an idea of the power of naming what you want, let me tell you what happened to me when I decided to name what I want. Through my dad's involvement in the strategic planning of legal cases, I became familiar with the legal profession and I absolutely loved it. I have known for a long time that what I wanted to do when I got older was to go to law school. So as I was working through my life, in school and in extracurricular activities and pretty much everything that I did, I tried to keep that ultimate goal in mind. Now granted, sometimes I did not exactly work efficiently toward my long-range goal. I would often get off track by not studying. But I did keep my eye on my goal, and as a result, I was able to see the difference between things that helped me get there and things that would prevent me from getting there.

That focus ultimately led me to making some serious decisions in my life. I mentioned earlier that I changed high schools after my sophomore year. As hard as it was to make that decision, I did it in pursuit of my ultimate plan. The first school I went to really emphasized math and science. The school made you take something like six math and science courses and only one each in English and history. That is all well and good if you are good at math, interested in math, and plan to pursue a career in which math would be important. But I was not. I am a word person. I like using words. I would rather write than add. I figured I was wasting my time grinding through these math courses then because they weren't going to have anything to do with the rest of my life.

I am not suggesting that you don't need to do your math homework, but for me, there was no need to constantly do calculus and trigonometry and every other form of voodoo manipulation of numbers you can imagine. Because I had a clear goal in mind, I made the decision to change schools because I was spending so much of my time and energy learning the math, which I would never use, when I could and should be spending that time developing a vocabulary that I could and would use later in life.

You will always have similar decisions to make about choices in your life. Your decisions may be about school or even summer jobs. Because I know I want to be a lawyer when I get older, a summer job at a hospital may not be the best fit. It doesn't help me move toward my goal. It doesn't give me experience toward what I want to do. Instead, I will go apply and get the same job at a law firm because that does help me move toward my goal. Every detail that you can know about your long-range goal in life will help you to get there quicker and more successfully.

IT'S OKAY TO WANT

As you go through the process of naming what you want for your life, it's okay to say, "I want this for me." If someone gives you grief about your dreams for the future, don't listen. The people who stay stuck are those who refuse to dream. It is important to want more in your life and it is important that you make yourself a priority. Don't be shy about saying that

WHAT I WANT
MULTIPLE CHOICE

☐ RECOGNITION ☐ SUCCESS ☐
☐ FAME ☐ RICHES ☐ MAKE THE TEAM
☐ RELIGION ☐ HAPPINESS ☐ COLLEGE
☐ INTEGRITY ☐ INDEPENDENCE ☐ FULFILLMENT

you want something special for yourself, whether it is a special feeling, a special experience, or a special item. And what's more, don't be shy about working on it, asking for help, and using everything you can to get your constructive goal.

It's like my granddad always used to say: "You will never catch a fish if your hook isn't in the water." Same here. You will never get something you don't ask for. Even if you are just asking yourself for it, you have to ask.

Once you know exactly what you want, don't forget the second half of this law: claiming what you have named. Knowing what you want is worthless if you are not willing to step up and take it once you have gotten there. You have to have the guts and the resolve to say, "This is my destiny." It sounds lofty. But you make it your reality. You say, "This is my goal, I am here, I have earned my way to it, and I'm going to take it. I won't let anybody make me feel selfish or guilty for stepping up and claiming what I have worked hard to get." You have to be willing to say, "I have worked my ass off to get here and I am taking what I have earned. I am going to claim it. I am going to claim it for me."

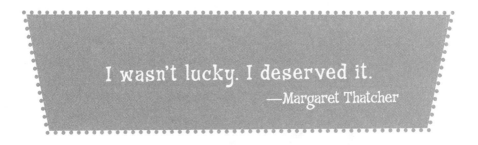

I wasn't lucky. I deserved it.
—Margaret Thatcher

Understand that you are not stealing anything; you've earned this, and you deserve it. You have worked hard, applied the laws of life, and now it is your turn to step up and take what you have earned.

There's a practical reason for stepping up. This is a competitive world in which we live; if you don't take what is yours, somebody else will. Why would you want to make it easier for them? Why leave your windows open for thieves? Once you have strength and resolve enough to believe that you deserve what it is that you want, then and only then will you be bold enough to say, "It is my time, it is my turn; this is for me, and I claim it."

So it's time to get going, to lead a life full of challenges and aspirations, excitement and happiness. It's time to take the journey that you are meant to take. And remember to enjoy the journey. As has been said many times, the game of life is not about the final score but about the playing. It's not about the destination but about the trip. If you live life to its fullest, whatever that kind of life is, then you have become a winner. You have become one of those rare few who "get it."

LIGHTBULBS

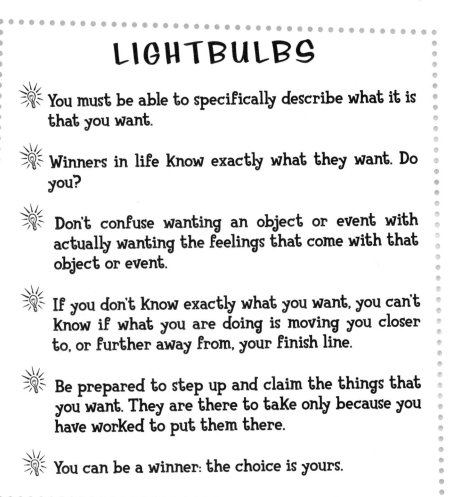

- You must be able to specifically describe what it is that you want.

- Winners in life know exactly what they want. Do you?

- Don't confuse wanting an object or event with actually wanting the feelings that come with that object or event.

- If you don't know exactly what you want, you can't know if what you are doing is moving you closer to, or further away from, your finish line.

- Be prepared to step up and claim the things that you want. They are there to take only because you have worked to put them there.

- You can be a winner: the choice is yours.

CONCLUSION

We are the people our parents warned us about.

—Jimmy Buffett

WELL, THERE YOU HAVE IT: THE TEN LIFE LAWS translated so that "normal people" can understand them. If you are reading this (and you didn't skip ahead), then congratulations! You have created a great chance for yourself to have more of what you want, now and in the future. You should be really excited, and I bet you are.

But I'm not done—not just yet. As I have mentioned a time or two in previous chapters, I interviewed lots of kids in preparing this book. I think that I have pretty much covered the topics that seemed to come up most often. But just to be sure I don't miss something that matters to you (and because I'm not ready to sign off yet), in closing, I want to refocus on some particularly hot areas. We have dealt with some of these topics in the context of the ten Life Laws, but I want to be extra clear on certain points that I think will be big deals in the next several months of your life.

Two things: First, I intend to discuss these few topics in reference to the Life Laws that apply, but I will confess that my personal opinions and values are likely to creep in, so take what I say as just one person's point of view. In other words, if you think I am full of crap, then proceed with caution. Even so, I hope my thoughts will stimulate yours even if you disagree. Second, I intend to be brief and to the point, but that doesn't mean I'm going to tell you what you want to hear, either. And most of all, I won't lecture you like your parents. Let's start with three topics that always get and hold the attention of young and old alike.

SEX, DRUGS, AND ROCK AND ROLL

Sex

"Sounds good to me!" you're thinking. "The most fun you can have without laughing . . ." Right? Now, obviously, whether you do or don't have sex is clearly up to you. I'm not saying it necessarily should be, but in this day and time it is. Your parents can't watch you 24/7. It is your body and your choice. I'm certainly not the person to preach at you and tell you what to do in your personal life. But I do want you to make a decision, whatever that decision may be. Let's face it, this is a tough subject to talk about with your parents. It's tough for you and for them. Embarrassing is what it is. A buddy of mine told me that his "birds and bees" talk with his dad consisted of his old man yelling, "Hey! Cut that out!" That was it. Another friend said he learned everything he knew about sex from the first girl he had it with. On-the-job training, so to speak! Not a good thing! Don't be a moron here. You can mess up your life big-time in a hurry if you don't think about the possible consequences of your choices and actions.

Make no mistake—as Life Law Two says, when you choose the behavior, you do choose the consequences. That's the problem with "grown-up" behavior; if it goes wrong, it can go way wrong. There is an old saying: "Every rose has its thorn." And sex is no exception.

Almost all thirteen- to eighteen-year-olds who I talked with who had had sex in junior high or high school said that within a very short time afterward they regretted it. "It seemed like a good idea at the time," they said. "Everyone was doing it, and I thought we were in love." Others felt it was simply "the next thing to do" and had no big issue with it, good or bad.

There are clearly pros and cons to any issue, and this one is no exception. On the positive side, it can be fun, feel good at the time, and make you feel closer to your girlfriend or boyfriend. Having sex can make you feel pretty grown up and certainly give you a feeling of independence. When everything is going okay it can seem like a no-brainer. Those are the positives, at least from one perspective. That's the rose.

Now for the thorns. I am sure you have heard all the negatives before, but here is a review of the sexual lowlights. First, you can get pregnant—a big, big side effect that, as you now know, can change or destroy your life. Think about waking up one morning with that little bit of news. A friend of mine has a T-shirt that sums up my second point pretty well (how's that for a credible source of info—a T-shirt!). Anyway, it says:

Love is fickle, it goes away
But HERPES is here to stay!

On the back it says:

And AIDS will freakin' kill you!

Bottom line: You can't wash that stuff off! There's no pill you can take and no Oops! or do-overs here. You create your own experience and you teach people how to treat you. Think that through and see what it tells you about the price being charged against your body. Ugly, but true.

It's your decision, but I encourage you to think ahead about how you will feel if, in fact, the worst happens and you get pregnant, infected, or dumped. Be honest with yourself. Don't be in denial about a possible downside, because it's real, very real. Consider your decision morally, socially, behaviorally, physically, and emotionally. It is not a simple decision because once you do it you cannot undo it. Did you get that? *You cannot undo it.* Know this above all else: It is your body and you have the right to say *no!* It's up to you. Just don't make the decision on the spur of the moment and don't lie to yourself about the possibilities.

Drugs

I promised I wouldn't lecture, but if you are doing drugs, we ought to start charging you dues to the Dumb-Ass Club. That behavior is nuts and you need to quit, and quit now. (At least you don't have to guess where I stand on this issue.) Remember Life Law Three: People do what works. Obviously you are getting some payoff if you are doing drugs. You have to get real and ask yourself if whatever the payoff is, is it really what you want, or are you hiding from your life? I mean, think about it—can something you swallow, smoke, snort, or inject really fix your problems? No way! We may wish it could, but it can't. Do you think it prepares you for or gets you closer to anything on your goals list? No way!

You, having learned what you have from this book so far, may now be asking yourself how in the world you ever got started down this path. (At least I hope you're asking yourself that.) I have learned that we often start or pick up habits for one reason, yet continue them for a completely different set of reasons. If you were doing drugs before you read this book, it was most likely because you were one of those who didn't get it. It was because you didn't have things going on in your life, you had no momentum, no goals and no plan to get them. You probably started doing drugs because you thought it was a good alternative, and to be honest, you had damn little else to focus on. It's my hope, however, that you are now becoming one of those who does get it and therefore you don't need that nasty stuff anymore. You do have plenty going on—like your whole life, for example! You didn't need drugs then; you sure as hell don't need them now.

I hope you will no longer rely on drugs and won't continue to hang out with people who do. Everybody I ever knew who did drugs did them because their friends did, or because it was the easy way to define themselves. It gave them some identity. The only criterion, the only price of admission to that group of losers, was doing the drugs. The participants could be short, tall, fat, skinny, smart, dumb, honest, or slimy. They could be clean or dirty, but they were in; they were accepted as long as they did drugs. Free pass, it seems, but, in fact, a very, very high price is being paid, and you are the one who has to pay it.

It is my hope that you will now require more of yourself and not just live half-baked, dazed, and confused. Use your power and your mind, not some chemical. You are better than that and you know it. When you stop buzzing your brain and start thinking and taking pride in yourself, I'm betting it won't be very long at all before you look back on your "drug days" and say "How dumb was that?"

Rock and Roll

Love it! Turn it up! Music is great. I play mine loud! My dad always says, "Son, you're going to go deaf." I say, "Huh?"

POPULARITY AND PEER PRESSURE

Look, here's my thinking; you can disagree if you want to. I like me just fine, and if somebody, right out of the blue, decides not to include me or like me, it's okay with me. I will decide how I feel about me. I won't give that power to anyone else, and I mean nobody: not friends, girlfriends, family—nobody. I will work on a friendship with them, I will put in some effort and energy if I happen to like a particular person, but I won't beat myself up if they don't like me and I won't dance in the streets if they do. I don't say this defensively; it's just how I feel. Popularity is not all it is cracked up to be. I've been on both sides of that deal, and I was the same person either way. If I had a choice between having one loyal, honest, good friend, or ten "cool" kids who might not have those qualities, I'll take my one good friend any day of the week. I'm not even two years out of high school and I can tell you that I don't care one bit about these kids who I may have at one point thought were God's gift to the world. I have gone on to other things in my life; they have gone on to other things in their life. So it goes. No big deal. The "cool kids" are that way only because you and maybe some other people decided to label them as such. They are no different from you. You shouldn't tear them down in your mind and heart, but neither should you build them up.

And let's talk about this peer pressure BS. I'll bet this conversation has happened in every house in America:

> **You or Me:** "Mommmm, everybody's doing it. I don't know why I can't!"
>
> **Mom:** "I guess if they were all jumping off a bridge, you would want to jump off, too!"

I hate to admit it, but "everybody else is doing it" is a pretty stupid reason for doing anything. Look, think for yourself. Choose for yourself. One thing I have painfully learned is that you and your friends may do stupid stuff together, but you will pay the price for that stupidity alone.

What are we thinking? If we are caving in to peer pressure to do drugs, have premarital sex, blow off school, defy our parents, or just generally be pissed off because "everybody is doing it," we have stopped thinking. My opinion is that if you are going to be independent, if you are going to be your own person, then do that. Don't just say you are being independent and being your own person. I mean truly, no kidding, bottom line, be who you really are. That leads me to my final topic.

SELF-ESTEEM AND SELF-IDENTITY

I don't care who you are or how accomplished you have become; everybody has self-doubts. Everybody at some point has doubts about themselves, their worth, and value. I am bringing this up because everybody I talked to spoke about it, so I know it is important to you.

Here's the deal: It really is true that there never, ever in the history of the world has been and never, ever in the future of the world will be another you. You are an original. God made one form and then broke the mold. When you think about that, it is really pretty neat. Wouldn't it be a waste if you never, ever really figured out who you were and never, ever let yourself be that unique person because you were so busy kissing somebody else's ass or were caught up in rebelling or defying the authorities in your life to the point that you forgot about being who you really are?

Having the only one of anything in this world is pretty cool when you think about it. And you have the only one of you. Treat yourself as the treasure you really are. If somebody is dogging on you, don't let them convince you that you are not pretty damn special, because you are.

And when you start comparing yourself to others, as we all do at one time or another, let me tell you a little secret I figured out. We all know the whole truth about ourselves, good or bad. We know our weak points and our flaws. But if you are like me, you probably hide them pretty well. So does everybody else. What that means is that when you are comparing yourself to someone else, you are comparing your true self to the other person's social mask. You are going to lose that contest 100 out of 100 times. You may be standing there feeling like crap because you know your parents fight like cats and dogs and that your family is having such financial trouble that you may have to sell your house. But you are comparing that truth to some other kid's "everything is fine at my house" social mask. The truth is, others may be going through way more hell than you ever thought about.

All I am saying to you here is to believe in yourself, be who you are, and don't put yourself down in comparison to other people. You have the potential for a great life ahead of you, but it is up to you to live it.

That's my story and I am sticking to it.

Jay McGraw grew up in Dallas, Texas. He is currently a student at the University of Texas at Austin. Jay enjoys spending time with his girlfriend, Jennifer, and his younger brother, Jordan. Playing basketball, piloting small planes, and scuba diving are his favorite hobbies.